FRANCHISE ✓ALIDATOR

Questions You Should Ask to Avoid Financial Ruin

Donald Averitt, CFE

About the Author

Donald Averitt, CFE is a 25+ year franchise veteran and Certified Franchise Executive (CFE) as certified by the Institute of Certified Franchise Executives, sponsored by the International Franchise Association (IFA). He is very passionate about the franchise industry and in helping prospective franchisees during their discovery process. He spent 17 years of his career at International Center for Entrepreneurial Development (ICED), where he served as Vice President of Franchise Development. ICED was formally the parent company for eight franchise brands, with over 1500 locations in 22 countries. ICED was founded by IFA Man of the Year and IFA Hall of Fame member, the late F.C. "Bud" Hadfield. Mr. Averitt was fortunate to have been mentored by Mr. Hadfield before and during his tenure at ICED. His first job after Texas A&M University was as Director of Operations – Kwik Kopy Corporation, the predecessor of ICED. As Director of Operations at Kwik Kopy, he was responsible for each location getting open during an era in which Kwik Kopy was opening between 100-150 stores per year. Mr. Averitt worked in a franchise that his parents owned in Richmond, Virginia, gaining exposure to the "owners side" of the franchise world. The balance of Mr. Averitt's career was as VP Franchise Development with some other national franchise brands and most recently with Safeguard, a wholly-owned subsidiary of Deluxe Corp (NYSE:DLX), where he contributed to over $100 million in mergers and acquisitions. Mr. Averitt lives with his wife in Henderson, Nevada where he consults with independent business owners who wish to convert their business to a franchise. He speaks on the subject of Franchising and is promoting his book "*Franchise Validator – What Questions You Should Ask to Avoid Financial Ruin*".

Mr. Averitt contributes on the subject of Franchising in social Media. He also maintains two Websites on franchising with an emphasis on validation:
http://www.FranchiseValidator.com and
http://www.FranchiseNinja.com

He can be reached via email at: Donald@franchisevaildator.com

He is also very grateful to the contributing authors:

Lane Fisher, who wrote the chapter entitled – *"Questions You Should Ask Your Franchise Attorney"* (Chapter 6).

Rod Bristol, CFE, who wrote the chapter entitled – *"Questions You Should Ask Your CPA/Financial Advisor"* (Chapter 7).

Jenny Childs, CFE, who wrote the chapter entitled – *"Questions You Should Ask Your Franchise Consultant"* (Chapter 8).

Mr. Averitt is also grateful to two other franchise experts who have given their gracious permission to reprint valuable and worthwhile articles that they had contributed to online social media. Thank you to:

Terry Powell, CFE *("Three Questions You Should Ask Before Deciding Which Franchise is Best for You").*

Dr. John P. Hayes. *("Buy a Franchise With Confidence Using These 4 Questions).*

A brief bio and their qualifications are at the end of each chapter that they authored / contributed.

Table of Contents

Introduction / About This Book

There are numerous books on the subject of franchising, many of which I have read. There is certainly no doubt that there are many qualified authors on the subject. I have the utmost respect for those qualified, experienced writers who have tried to share their experience with you in order to help you in your discovery process. However, after seeing what is available on the subject of franchising, I can assure you that this book is different. I can also say that no single book on the subject, including this one, will cover everything you need to know about purchasing a franchise. There are books that describe every step of the process. Whether it is seven steps, nine steps or 15 or 20, I have seen books that differently describe the number of steps, but still explain the same process! I hope that this is not your *first* book on buying a franchise because I do not go into detail describing *the process* itself. Nor do I explain *where* to find information on different franchises. There are already a ton of books that address those subjects and any good Internet search will get you more information than you can possibly process. If you haven't found out by now, once you stick your toe in the water, there will be no shortage of brokers, consultants and franchise brands looking to get your attention.

I feel uniquely qualified to have made some assumptions about your search for a franchise. I think you know *where* to look for information. And if any of the franchise brands that you contact interest you, you will automatically be transported into the process, most likely without even knowing it. There are two things I have seen about prospective franchisees. First, they haven't done enough initial soul searching and inward reflection to know if this is really what they want to do. And secondly, they do not know what questions to ask during the process.

In my 25+ years in the franchising industry, I have sold franchises (awarded licenses) to hundreds of happy (and not-so-happy) franchisees. Considering that the conversion rate is .5-2% of the number of prospects one must talk to in order to actually sell a franchise, this translates into interviewing tens of thousands of prospective franchisees! And what I have found is that the franchise sales representative is more than adequately prepared for what he is going to say because he has already done it thousands of times. And on the other end of the phone, the prospect is woefully unprepared, doesn't know what to say or know what questions to ask. Nor does he know what questions to be prepared to answer. And that is the purpose of this book.

The chapters have been broken down into different steps of the process in which you need to be prepared to ask questions. I have tried to include the appropriate questions at each stage of the process that you *should* be prepared to ask. Most of which you may have thought of, or many of which will be questions that you would think of after you hang up the phone and wish you would have asked. Of course, you cannot ask *all* of these questions. Some of them may not apply to you, and many of them will not apply to the franchise brand(s) of which you are investigating. But definitely all of the questions are meant to stimulate your thought process and remind you of some questions you may not have even thought of.

So, after reading the book, and the franchise sales representative asks, "do you have any questions for me?" you will least have an idea what to say and what to ask.

CHAPTER 1

Questions you should ask yourself (and your family)

"To thine own self be true, and it must follow, as the night the day, thou canst not then be false to any man"
—**Shakespeare** (from Hamlet)

Regardless of why you have chosen to investigate the purchase of a franchise, the assumption is that you are at a certain stage in your life at which you have certain experience and success. The purchase of a franchise is a significant investment...usually thousands, if not hundreds of thousands, of dollars. So, you have management experience. You want to get out of the corporate life. The past several years, you have had your own office, a nice comfortable chair, an assistant and an 8 to 5 workweek with weekends off. Vacations, holidays and bonuses are taken for granted. Nice. The first question you must ask yourself is how important are these things to you? Because in your new franchise venture, you may have an office, but probably not an assistant, and you definitely will not be working just 8 to 5 (probably more like 12 or more hours per day). Weekends off? Forget it. Taking a vacation or bonus money in the first year is probably out of the question, also. If you were in management in your previous position, you probably just called someone when the toilet was stopped up. Now consider that when the toilet is stopped up in your new business, you will be the one grabbing the plunger to get things flowing again!

Are you okay with this? Depending on which opportunity you choose, you might be hiring an entire staff of young high school students. History has proven they are not the most reliable employees. When one (or 2 or more) call in sick, or don't show up at all, you will be the one filling in for them. Are you okay with this? Better yet, are your wife and family okay with you spending all your time at the new business? So, the following questions are prepared so that you will have an idea of what type of opportunity would be best for you. Also are you franchise material? Knowing that you will be a good fit, financially, culturally and mentally will make you a much better franchisee.

Do you have the intestinal fortitude to be in business for yourself?

When you decide to buy a franchise, there are certain character traits you must possess. Owning and operating your own business requires motivation, willingness to work hard, wisdom, money, people skills, communication, knowledge and experience, family support, perseverance and being level-headed, among many other things, such as complete trust in the franchisor.

Motivation is the "unbridled desire" that drives us no matter what...that burning fire to succeed to do whatever is necessary to make the franchise work. What is your motivation in starting your own business? Is it that you have never been paid adequately for your skills and knowledge? Are you frustrated with corporate politics? Are you frustrated with the hours or commute? Managing incompetent people? It's that desire which motivates people to start their businesses and "stick to it" through good times and bad.

Willingness to work hard. Running a franchise is *not* a nine-to-five job. Working long hours and weekends are not unusual, especially in the beginning (and probably on an ongoing basis, as well).

If you are already motivated, it's **wisdom** that helps you stay grounded as you work long hours without complaining. Staying with the job at hand, until it is done, it is what you will need to get along with your employees, how you will handle money and the daily crises with self-control and composure. All these obstacles take mental fortitude, to accept the hard work and occasional challenges to do whatever it takes to make your dreams come true. When you own your own business, you need to be able to see the "big picture", yet also tend to the daily minutiae. Set a series of small and large, immediate and long-term goals so you can easily chart the progress to achieve your dreams while being practical and sensible. Overcoming daily challenges while staring in the face of adversity...that's wisdom.

Starting a business takes **money**. Only you can determine how much you can put into your business without jeopardizing your household financial health and future planning. Sacrifices are expected when opening / buying a business. Remember that starting a business requires not only working capital, but also *living* capital. How much sacrifice are you going to make in your standard of living to get your business off the ground? With your spouse/family, you must discuss and agree on how much of your net worth you are comfortable in investing. You will also need to determine which of your assets (cash in the bank, savings, 401(k), stocks, home equity, insurance cash-value) that you will need to convert to liquid cash in order to meet the financial qualification requirements that your bank or franchisor may impose.

Are you a **people person**? Effectively dealing (and communicating) with your franchisor, suppliers, employees and customers is necessary in being a successful franchisee. To be in business for yourself you will need to be able to get along with people...especially in a franchise model.

Franchisees **communicate** often and openly with the representatives at every level of the franchise home office. The more information and ideas that are shared, the more help the franchisor will have in developing new programs and products/services for the rest of the network. It is absolutely essential to work effectively with field personnel who can share their broad wealth of knowledge in how other franchisees have experienced success. They are always willing to share solid information from trusted and valued associates, as well as their own experiences. One can never communicate too much. Don't assume that someone already knows something. Better to over communicate than to let something fall through the cracks because it wasn't adequately communicated.

You need to have **knowledge and experience** in your industry. You will need to be **willing to listen and** learn. You will need to know your business and industry inside and out. No matter how much previous business experience you have, there's always a lot to learn in any franchise because the franchisor wants you to learn and implement *their* system. However, franchise training doesn't cover *everything* you need to know. You also need to know what your specific skill set is. It would be very wise to take a personal skill inventory. Many companies offer personality assessments that measure skills, passions/desires, and aptitudes. Many consulting firms use this assessment tool to match a prospect to one of the franchise offerings in their portfolio. And many franchisors use these tools to determine if you are a fit for their brand. Sometimes, certain franchises require a certain skill set and/or aptitude in a certain skill to award you a franchise. For example, if you are investigating a B2B franchise, (business-to-business – where you have very little walk-in traffic, but sales rely on personal sales efforts), you cannot be shy or have a fear of sales and rejection. Are you a sales person, creative, good money manager or handy with your hands? You need to know what your strengths are. Remember that a franchise is a proven system. Their training program will teach you their system. And good, quality franchisors will have invested significant time and money in a training program that teaches basic competence in their industry and a basic knowledge in the way they specifically want things done to ensure consistency across the system/network. While training may cover the fine details of a specific system, the franchisor may leave the general business and management fundamentals up to you. You should take an honest look at your skill set and evaluate your level of competence in such fields as finance, accounting, HR/employee management, legal, operations, marketing and advertising. Knowing what your weaknesses are will give you the information you need to strengthen your knowledge/competence in those areas.

Be **level-headed.** Are you able to make decisions reasonably and intelligently? Can you handle stress, daily pressure, and constant conflicts carefully and consciously? You cannot lack composure because you will make poor decisions. If you are quick-tempered, you may put success at risk by alienating both customers and employees alike.

Perseverance is a necessary trait for any franchisee. When a dirty job needs to be done, a bad employee needs counseling (or to be fired), or a when a good customer's order gets messed up and needs to be fixed, you will need to see that it gets done. When you face challenges, you must draw on your experience, wisdom and maturity to make the best possible business decisions. It takes perseverance and determination to be successful!

Ability and willingness to follow a system. One of the most important things you get when you are awarded a franchise is their *system*. A tried and proven blueprint for success. Following it is absolutely essential. This is not negotiable. If you think you might want to get creative and do things your way, you will be frustrated in a franchise system, and you should probably consider starting your own independent business. True entrepreneurs innovate; find new niches and new ways to do things. If you are one who questions things, want to change anything to do with a product, you will not be happy in a franchise system. In short, a franchisee needs to blindly accept things as they are.

The "system" you buy from the franchisor is contained in the operations manuals. It is enforced through the franchise agreement. This is the "blueprint for success" in which *all* franchisees operate within any given franchise system. It cannot be stressed enough that there is not much flexibility when you own a franchise. The training program TRAINS you from the operations manual. You OPERATE the franchise by the manual. It is enforced through the Franchise Agreement. You AGREE to the terms of the agreement. The agreement is a long-term agreement. You will abide by the terms expressed in the agreement or risk losing your franchise, or at the minimum, the right to renew your franchise. You will operate your franchise as the franchisor wishes...even when you disagree from within. This takes an even higher level of maturity to operate under these conditions.

The ability to take criticism graciously. It is in the franchisor's main interest to require everyone follow the system consistently. They want the customer to have the same uniform experience regardless of city or location. If the franchisor thinks you need to implement a new system, or increase sales or enforce a brand standard, or if you are ignoring policies and certain practices that might be taking your franchise in a different direction, you will certainly hear from them (and it won't be a good day).

You will need to have a **complete trust in your franchisor.** You will need to (almost blindly) believe in and support your franchisor's system, policies, products and/or services. You must constantly remind yourself that they receive royalties from the franchisees, so it is in their best interest to help franchisees build the largest, most successful business possible. The more successful you are, the more successful they are! The franchisor should be seeking every possible path to help you maximize that potential. This will often result in developing new policies, methods and products for you to utilize in the operation of your franchise. In the spirit of cooperation, you will accept these new products and programs, even when you disagree with them.

Family Support

Strong family support is not only invaluable; it is absolutely necessary. I have personally seen many families fall apart because of the decision to go into business. This is especially true when the decision to go into business doesn't have complete "buy in" from the complete family and even more especially if family money helps finance the business. You will need support for your idea from your family regardless if they will be working in the business or not. There should also be agreement that if the family is working together in the business on a daily basis, that there should be a rule to "leave the work at the office" so to speak. Accounts payable should not be discussed over the evening meal.

Your family will need to make sacrifices over the next several years. Your hours will be long and irregular, you won't have weekends to go on trips and outings, you may miss meals and social events, and in general, you will have less time for family. Your family also needs to know that you no longer get a regular paycheck. You won't be paid until all the other expenses and employees have been paid. That means that in some months there may be very little, if any, money left over for them. And even when you do have good months, that surplus money will need to be put back into the business. Growing (and expanding) the business is one of the most costly things to do. The business bank account cannot be used like a piggy bank. You should have a family meeting with all stake holders to get buy-in from everyone who will be affected *before* you embark on your new venture.

Before you begin researching a specific franchise:

Ask yourself:
- Why are you looking at this specific brand / business?
- Why are you so confident that it is the best choice for you and your family?
- You did not choose it just to satisfy your ego?
- Or because it was glamorous?
- That someone else (or *anyone else*) did not talk you into it?
- You are prepared for the bad days and hard work that will be necessary to endure to make your new business successful?
- Will your franchise be taking a considerable amount of time away from your family? And how do all family members feel about that?
- Are you aware that self-employment, including franchising, often requires harder work and longer hours than employed positions?
- Do you have a decisive mindset and could you make the decision in the first place to step out of employment and into self-employment?
- Are your family and friends supportive about your plans to start your own business? Will you enjoy working with them if they are to serve as employees?
- Are they in complete agreement?
- Are you and your spouse ready to make the necessary sacrifices in the way of money and time to successfully operate the business?

- Will the loss of company benefits, including retirement plans, be outweighed by the potential monetary and sense of accomplishment that would result in owning your own business?
- Have you made a complete, thorough written balance sheet of assets and liabilities, plus liquid resources?
- Will your savings last for at least one year after your initial investment and allowing for a one year drop in household income?
- Do you have a back-up plan of additional resources including friends and/or relatives who might be able to loan you money in the event your initial funding proves inadequate?
- Regardless of what the representatives of the franchise tell you, you do realize that most franchises do not break even for at least a year after opening?
- Will your spouse (or other family member) continue to work their current job during ramp up, or initial start-up phase?
- Do you enjoy working with others?
- Comfortable leading and managing other people?
- Do you have the skill set, background and character traits necessary to be successful in business?
- Do you possess a flexible work mentality and can you focus on different jobs as may be required and multitask effectively?
- Can you deal with high-pressure and stressful situations effectively?
- Do you usually have a positive mindset, as well as plenty of drive, determination and perseverance?
- Do you have the necessary financial resources? Working capital *and* living capital? If not, where are you going to get the necessary capital?
- Do you have an excellent credit rating / score?

- Are you prepared for working long, hard hours?
- Are you and your spouse confident that your marriage/ relationship is strong and stable enough to handle the emotional and physical strain involved in operating a franchise, caused by long hours and tedious administrative chores?
- Will your family members, particularly your children, suffer from your absence for several years while you build the business?
- Are you prepared to give up any autonomy, or independence in exchange for the advantages of owning a franchise?
- Can you operate within an established system even if you think you have a better way?
- Can you follow a system, but still think "outside the box"?
- Are you open to receiving guidance and support, especially if it does not necessarily reflect your own views or opinions?
- Have you honestly evaluated the franchise you desire and concluded that you would enjoy running this business for several years or until retirement?
- Are you physically in great condition? Have you had a physical?
- Do you enjoy working with others? Managing others / Are you a "people person"?
- Which are you most comfortable with – managing just a couple of employees or large staff?
- Would you want to work five days a week or do you want your business to be open seven days a week?
- Are you a morning or night person?
- Are you a self-starter and a disciplined worker?
- Can you see things through to the end even with lots of challenges?
- Can you accept that decisions will not always go your way?

- Can you take constructive instruction and criticism from authority figures and experts?
- Can you ask for help when you need it?
- Are you willing and able to thoroughly research project before jumping in?
- Are you motivated to work hard, long hours every day?
- Are you willing to accept that there is not going to be instant success?
- Can you handle emergencies and meet deadlines?
- Do you have a high tolerance for risk?
- Do you have the ability to work smoothly and communicate effectively with your franchisor, your employees, suppliers and customers?
- Have you asked your friends and relatives for a candid, honest opinion as to whether they think you are mature enough, possess the skill set and are emotionally, physically and mentally able to run a business?
- Do you have a capable, willing person to take over your business in the even you die or become disabled/incapacitated?
- Can you learn new skills and procedures quickly?
- Do you have the technical expertise or knowledge for the business you are considering?
- Are you comfortable using new technology?
- Are you comfortable that you have to sell yourself and your products and services to complete strangers?
- Do you have basic accounting and/or bookkeeping skills?
- Can you write a business plan?
- Are you comfortable with sales and marketing? Are you good at it?
- Are you comfortable in networking situations?
- What is it that you really want to achieve in this business? Money, personal satisfaction, get out of your existing job, be your own boss?

- Have you considered what type of business will allow you to maximize your existing personal and business skills?
- Do you understand that a franchise does not bring the guarantee of success, but is more likely to be successful if you work hard and followed the proven business model that a franchisor provides?
- Are you going into this with an exit strategy?

I have always felt that the answers to the questions you ask yourself are the most important. The questions you ask the franchisor, their franchisees, your attorney and your financial advisor are easier than the ones you ask yourself. Only after you have the answers to these difficult questions, should you continue.

CHAPTER 2

What You Should Look For in a Franchisor

"Sometimes your best investments are the ones you don't make."
—Donald Trump

Finding the right franchise begins with *you*. If you asked yourself the hard questions from the last chapter and have had an honest, internal look at yourself, and are still interested in investing in a franchise, then the next step is to inquire at the franchises that interest you the most.

Always research a franchise before you buy. Too many people buy a franchise based on emotion and then realize that it was a mistake when it is too late, but a little research could have prevented a disaster!

It is important to pursue a brand that interests you. But do not limit your research to only one franchise even if you have a strong inclination to that brand and think it's the one you want to buy. It is also important to know what level of support you will need or want. As I mentioned previously, just because they make a great pizza, or hamburger, does not mean that they are a good franchisor. Before looking at specific franchises, determine what you expect from the franchisor. Determine if there is a particular service/need that is lacking in your community. Then evaluate to determine if this is something you can "get your arms around". Will it generate enough income while improving your quality of life and allow you to have fun while doing it? Are there franchise brands available in your marketplace that you can afford and have a proven system for success? Or will you be an "early adapter" in a new franchise that will allow for a "ground floor" opportunity. New franchises will allow the most flexibility in the operation of your franchise, but also will not have the level of support that you might need (or want).

Actually, it would be good advice to compare two or three franchise systems with your established personal and business models. And even a few franchises that are in totally different industries. A great way to do this is to disguise each businesses' name and then compare their attributes to your ideal business model. This is exactly how a franchise broker/consultant offers one of the strongest ways to help you in comparing like models and differing industries.

Before you begin researching thoroughly, narrow your search to only two or three brands. It would be impossible to research and compare too many brands. It would also be too time-consuming and overwhelming.

Consider your own tastes and preferences, but be realistic. Don't expect the franchisor to do the daily work and make everyday decisions required to run your business. It's your job to work hard and make your business succeed! However, if a franchisor can't meet certain standards, you should seriously consider NOT becoming a franchisee in that system.

You should look for franchise brands that:

- Are recognizable leaders in their given industry;
- Have a proven record of success;
- Can demonstrate levels of competency and mastery in training, support, advertising and marketing, financial and accounting;
- Do not penalize you for increased sales. And allow for unlimited earnings;
- Offer the quality of life for you and your family in which you are searching;
- Is affordable with your available resources.
- Requires an amount of time necessary to grow the business with which you are comfortable being away from your spouse and family;
- Offers personal, developmental and financial growth;
- Offers a product and/or service that has a proven, sustainable marketplace demand;
- Offers a clear vision of their future and how you would participate in that vision;
- Are ethical and give you an internal "gut check" feeling with which you are comfortable;

Questions to consider in researching a franchise brand:

- Do they have a proven, successful system developed over many years that can be easily taught to the franchisee?

- Are they committed to the franchise model in distributing products to the ultimate customer through the franchise network? Or are they more interested in selling more franchises? You don't want to consider a franchise that is selling products through several channels, such as Online, corporate sales, National Accounts, grocery stores and company–owned stores. You don't want to compete against your own franchisor!

- Are you in sync with your franchisor's vision? It is very important for you to believe in the future of the franchise. Businesses need to change to stay competitive, and it's important to feel comfortable with the direction that you (and the franchise) are going.
- Do you see a sustained demand for the products and services of the franchise? Five, 10 and 20 years from now?
- Is the quality of products and services in the marketplace perceived as good, or high quality?
- Do they have strong name recognition and/or excellent growth possibilities? Strong trademark / brand name is one of the most important ingredients of what you are buying. It is best to select a franchise with a well-established brand, although in some cases the greatest growth opportunities might be found in newer systems (that still has a *proven system for success*). There are trade-offs. But no matter how well known the company, a franchise should produce and market quality goods and services for which there is an established, sustained market demand.
- Do they have great growth potential, and does it compare favorably against the competition?
- Do they have strong support in the form of a great training program, assistance with site location, field visits, annual conferences and meetings with other franchisees?
- Do they have a clear vision for the future in which you are in agreement? Are they willing to change with the trends in the social and business marketplace?
- Do they have adequate human and financial resources to provide ongoing support to their franchise network? You don't want to see 300 franchised units but only 15 employees of which the majority is in the franchise sales staff. But if you saw a franchise system that has 300 units and 60 employees in different departments, that should represent excellent support. This will also be obvious in a

mature system vs. a new system with fewer locations.
- Does the business model not only work well as a franchise, but is actually better *because* of the franchising model?
- Do they place a high value on the success of their franchisees?

Answers to these questions will lead you to a plan for selecting the right franchise for you. These are questions that will help you identify the brands in which you might be a good fit and make an initial inquiry. "Franchise fit" is an important concept because it will determine how comfortable you are with their ideals and plans for the future.

3 Questions to Ask Before Deciding Which Franchise is Right for You

By Terry Powell, CFE
Nov 12, 2014

You may know that you're looking to move from Employment to Empowerment by taking the avenue of business ownership to achieve self-sufficiency, but do you really know what business opportunity is right for you? When looking at the franchise industry, there are various segments that call for several requirements and necessities from business owners in order to thrive. There are hundreds, probably even thousands of business opportunities out there, but not all of these opportunities are right for every entrepreneur.

Are all of the options overwhelming you and causing you to rethink your entrepreneurial dreams? Think again. Here I examine how to identify which business opportunities are right for you.

Three Questions to Ask before Choosing a Franchise Concept

1. "Why?"

One of the most integral things that an entrepreneur must do before choosing a franchise opportunity is ask themselves why they want to be a business owner. Do you want to achieve self-sufficiency? Do you want to build equity? Are you looking for a secondary source of income? Depending on how a prospective entrepreneur answers these questions, they will be better equipped to identify the opportunities that may or may not be the right fit for them. There's a reason why this is one of the first steps in the business coaching process that The Entrepreneur's Source offers. Once an entrepreneur is able to examine why he or she wants to invest in a franchise, then they will be better equipped to explore the possibilities and available options.

2. "How Involved Do I Want to Be?"

Although many individuals assume that franchise owners need to be ever-involved in their franchise business, this isn't always the case. With the growing popularity of semi-absentee businesses, not all franchise owners need to be invested in their franchise at all times. The semi-absentee business concept is a business that entrepreneurs can start on the side while they have another job or obligation, as opposed to a full-time franchise business, which requires your complete effort and wouldn't allow for you to do something else in addition. Depending on if a prospective franchise owner wants to be there full-time or on a semi-absent basis, then certain opportunities may be eliminated.

3. "Do I Need Help?"

Many entrepreneurs fall into the trap of naively thinking that they can do everything on their own, when in fact, they cannot. Even if you're not a first-time franchise owner or have vast knowledge of the franchising industry, it's wise to seek help when investing in a franchise. You may not need help with every aspect of opening your franchise, but consulting with a business coach can help an individual narrow down which models may be the most fitting for a prospective entrepreneur based on his or her Income, Lifestyle, Wealth and Equity (I.L.W.E.) goals and other factors that are sometimes overlooked when choosing a franchise concept. Although this step is commonly overlooked, it is almost always the most necessary for future franchise owners to ask themselves.

Terry Powell has 30 years in the Business Coaching profession and is always looking for new experiences and adventures as an entrepreneur. A leader and entrepreneur, Terry Powell, founded **The Entrepreneur's Source** (TES), a business coaching service, and developed AdviCoach, a coaching advisory service. Terry Powell was also a key player in the creation and success of Franchise-Match and FranchiseSearch, both resources for locating franchise prospects. Powell launched FranchsEsource Brands International in 2007.

Terry Powell's experience ranges from developing franchises to consulting and advising future franchise owners and entrepreneurs. Powell has earned his International Certified Franchise Executive Certification and is also a board member on the International Franchise Association's Diversity Institute.

CHAPTER 3

Now that you have found a franchise (or two or three)

"The greatest mistake you can make in life is to continually be afraid that you will make one"
—Elbert Hubbard

Now that you have identified a few franchise brands to become interested enough to start requesting information, it is highly recommended that you begin your search with a minimum of at least two, possibly as many as four, brands to investigate. Ideally, these would be opportunities for which you are best suited as a result from the answers to the questions you asked yourself (Chapter 1). When you request information, whether it be online, or with a phone call, or at a tradeshow, you will be sent information. The information may arrive in your home mailbox, or in your email inbox online. After your initial review, you will either call the franchise representative, or they will call you. Usually, in the very first phone call, they will only want to confirm that you have received the information and see if you've had a chance to review it yet. If you have, they will want to schedule the initial interview. They will ask you for a very minimum of 45 minutes to a maximum of two hours, usually depending on the size of the investment and complexity of the franchise model. The average initial interview is an hour.

What we are going to discuss in this chapter are the questions that you should be prepared to ask during and after the initial interview. It is assumed at this point, that you do not have the Franchise Disclosure Document, or FDD. We will devote the following chapter to questions you should ask the franchisor *after* you have had a chance to review the FDD. But for this chapter, we want to prepare you with questions you should have after the initial interview. As I mentioned in the introduction, the franchise representative will be completely and fully prepared for the interview. Remember, they do this several times a day all week long. They know exactly what questions they're going to ask you. They have a questionnaire in front of them and they will be asking you questions from the questionnaire. They are looking for things such as your work experience, how much money you made, how much money you have in the bank, your retirement fund, your wife's work experience, how much she has in her 401(k), what you liked about your last job, what you didn't like, your hobbies, when you're expecting to pay for your children's college education, how much debt you have, what your credit score is, what resources you are going to use to pay for the franchise, what additional resources you will have to live on, etc. etc.

After the interview, in which they have asked all the questions and you have done all the talking, they will ask you what questions you have for them. And the obvious question will be, "How much money can I make?" If the franchise does not contain an earnings claim in Item 19 of the FDD (more on this later), their reply will be, "well, I would love to discuss this with you, because there s nothing negative to hide. But as you may be aware, the franchise industry is highly regulated by the Federal Trade Commission (FTC), so I can't discuss that with you at this point. I will see to it that you will get this information through our franchisees and show you other ways to get this information. Do you have any other questions for me?" To which you will reply, "No".

So, now the franchisor has a lot of information about you. But how much more do you know about the franchise other than what is in their promotional material they sent to your house or your email box? Not much, really. It is usually at the end of this conversation that the franchise representative will send you the FDD. The FDD is a federally mandated document they must put in your hands after the first *meaningful* conversation and/or meeting. If you wish to pursue the franchise further, it is required they send you this document. In it, you will find everything you need to know about that franchise. With the one possible exception being how much money you can make (unless they actually make a Financial Performance Representation – FPR – in their Item 19 of the FDD). There are 23 items of disclosure in the first few pages of the FDD. This is for all franchises, all brands, regardless of how large or small, or how long in business. *ALL* franchises must comply with what is known as "The Rule". Again, we will reserve discussion of the FDD in another chapter. I just want you to be aware of the procedure after the first interview.

The purpose of this chapter is to give you some questions to ask of the franchise representative at the end of the first interview. Questions you should ask, but may not be aware of yet. Many of the obvious questions will be answered in the FDD. What I will try to give you at this point will be questions that are a normal "bridge" from the initial interview until you receive the FDD.

At the completion of the initial interview call (or meeting), the franchise representative will want to schedule the FDD follow-up call. This call will also take at least an hour, especially if you have thoroughly reviewed the document. It is from the FDD that you will have the most questions.

So, use the following checklist upon completion of the initial interview. It probably will not be necessary to ask every single question on the list. But there will be a core list of about 10-15 questions you should ask for now. Don't be surprised if the representative answers with "you will find the answer to that in the FDD." Prior to asking any questions of the sales representative/broker, you should designate which question(s) you want the answers to before you get the FDD. Knowing that you might get the answer in the FDD, you still might want an answer before you pursue the opportunity further. That is, ask *the most important questions TO YOU* to help you feel more comfortable with yourself after answering the questions of yourself from the previous chapters.

Use this checklist when conducting your own investigation of each franchise brand:

- How long have you been in business and for how long have you been offering franchises?
- How many units did you open last year? How many do you want to open this year? And next year?
- What is the size of this industry? Is it stable, growing or declining? What are the future predictions for growth?
- Exactly what can your franchise do for me that I cannot do if I were to open an independent business like this? What are the main advantages?
- How many employees do you have? How many in the franchise development (sales) department? How many in operations? And training? How many field support employees?
- How often do field support personnel visit franchisees?
- Do you have experienced, well-trained management in each department? That has done this before? (If yes, will I get a chance to meet them?)
- Can you please discuss the territory I will be given? Is it based on population? Number of homes? Number of businesses? Automobile traffic? Foot traffic? Is it exclusive?

- Will I be guaranteed to be the only franchise in my territory for the length of the contract? Can you sell other franchises in my market area?
- If you determine that my territory can have an additional franchise, will I get a right of first refusal? What about a right of first refusal for an adjacent territory?
- How much space do I need? Are sales a direct result of how much space I have? I assume that the financial model takes in the consideration a certain price per square foot for rent. If my market is higher than that, will that affect my chance of success?
- Will I need to lease my own space? Will the franchisor help with site selection? Can I lease (or sublease) from the franchisor?
- Do you offer financing for any part of the initial investment? If so, what are the terms?
- In the FDD, will there be an item 19 earnings claim? Is it for sales? Or gross profit margins? Net profits?
- Will you be giving me information on actual sales or forecasted sales? Actual profits or forecasted profits?
- Will you be able to provide numbers on actual profits and losses for specific franchisees in your system?
- What do you do with the franchise fee? Is most of it reinvested in acquiring other franchisees or is a good portion use for training and support of existing franchisees?
- Do you know the success rate of your franchisees? Or failure rate?
- Will there be a roster of existing franchisees with contact information in the FDD?
- Are there any restrictions on other products I may sell?
- How much of my inventory do I have to buy directly from you, the franchisor? Or your designated suppliers and vendors? Or can I buy from whomever I choose as long as

the standards are met? Are any of the products proprie-tary...do I have to buy these from you?

- Are all of the circumstances for termination covered in the FDD? If so, if I am forced to sell my franchise back to the parent company, will I be compensated for my equity/goodwill?
- What are the restrictions to use of franchise brand, logo and service marks? Will I need to get permission or ap-proval every time I want to advertise?
- Do I have the right to use all logos, trademarks, and trade names associated with this franchise?
- Can you provide me with the name and contact informa-tion for your most successful franchisees? And can you give me the names and contact information for the least successful franchisees?
- Can you discuss any existing, ongoing litigation? Will it be listed in the FDD?
- Can you discuss the training? Is it taken seriously? Do you have an exclusive training staff? Or does management of the company teach the classes?
- Who pays for training? What do I have to pay while in training?
- Are there any conditions for which I will be denied a renewal of the franchise? Can I be terminated without cause? And under what conditions can I terminate the agreement?
- Am I guaranteed an opportunity to renew my franchise agreement?
- When you fail to renew a franchise agreement what are the most common reasons?
- I understand that franchises can fail, also. What would you say are the most common reasons for failure within your franchise?

- If I cancel the franchise agreement before opening, will I get my franchise fee back?
- Will you help me with writing a business plan?
- How much flexibility is there in the operation of the business?
- How much do you offer to franchisees in personal development? Financial planning?
- What skills or personality traits are frequently found among your highest performing franchisees?
- Do you have a monitoring system? Is there benchmarking for use in comparison of our financial statements?
- When I contact the existing franchisees, what are they going to tell me?
- Will there be any surprises when I review the FDD?

Obviously, you should put a star beside the questions that are most important to you. Listen for how eager the representative is to get you off the phone. Does he have the answers to your most important questions? He probably won't know the answer to all of these, but he should promise to find out and get back to you. See how long it takes. If he "forgets" or doesn't call you back, this would certainly be a red flag! Remember, these are basically the "first round" of questions you will use to make your final decision. And again, it would be best if you investigated at least three opportunities. See how the representatives compare, and how the answers to your most important questions differ (or are the same).

Next, questions you should ask after review of the FDD.

CHAPTER 4

Questions You Should Ask After Review of the FDD

Believe nothing merely because you have been told it.
Do not believe what your teacher tells you merely
out of respect for the teacher. But whatsoever,
after due examination and analysis,
you find to be kind, conducive to the good, the benefit,
the welfare of all beings that doctrine ---- believe and cling to,
and take it as your guide.
—Buddha

Now that you have made your first inquiry into a franchise that appears to be an opportunity that you can afford and have fun operating, you should make yourself very familiar with two important documents in your research. They are: 1) the Franchise Disclosure Document (FDD) and 2) the Franchise Agreement. By learning more about both of these documents and the details they require, you will be better prepared to investigate potential franchise opportunities. This chapter discusses the questions you should be prepared to ask the franchisor after reviewing these documents. It will be every bit as important to prepare another list of questions to the existing franchisees after reviewing the FDD. The next chapter will address those questions.

The Franchise Disclosure Document (FDD)

First, let's discuss what the FDD is. It is an FTC-mandated document required of *all* franchisors to provide to each prospective franchisee interested in possibly buying their franchise. Direct off the FTC website:

RULE SUMMARY:
The Franchise Rule gives prospective purchasers of franchises the material information they need in order to weigh the risks and benefits of such an investment. The Rule requires franchisors to provide all potential franchisees with a disclosure document containing 23 specific items of information about the offered franchise, its officers, and other franchisees.

The purpose of the FDD is to provide prospective franchisees with information about the franchisor, the franchise system and the agreements they will need to sign so that they can make an informed decision. In addition to the disclosure part of the document, the FDD includes the actual franchise agreement as well as any other agreements the franchisee will be required to sign, along with the franchisor's financial statements. The FDD is designed to give you some of the information you need in order to make an informed decision about investing in a particular franchise. By law, a franchisor cannot sell a franchise until the franchisor has presented the prospective franchisee with a Disclosure Document (and allowed a mandatory 14 days to pass before any money can trade hands). In fact, 14 states require franchisors to register their FDDs with the state or to notify them that they will offer franchises before they begin to conduct any franchising activity in the state. It is not allowed to be a marketing piece. It cannot look "flashy". The text is to be in black-and-white and contain 23 items of disclosure. Regardless of what type of franchise it is, whether it is hamburgers, pizzas, painting, pest control or printing, *all* franchises must present their FDD in the same uniform style. Receipt of the FDD is governed by the "14-day rule." This is a cooling-off period in which franchisors must give prospective franchisees 14 days to think about their decision before they are allowed to sign the franchise agreement. All FDD's will uniformly contain:

Item 1.   Franchisor, Any Parents, Predecessors and Affiliates
Item 2.   Business Experience (of the principals of the Franchise)
Item 3.   Litigation
Item 4.   Bankruptcy
Item 5.   Initial Franchise Fees
Item 6.   Other Fees
Item 7.   Estimated Initial Investment
Item 8.   Restrictions on Sources of Products and Services
Item 9.   Franchisee's Obligations
Item 10.   Financing
Item 11.   Franchisor's Obligations (Assistance, Advertising, Computer Systems and Training)
Item 12.   Territory
Item 13.   Trademarks
Item 14.   Patents, Copyrights and Proprietary Information
Item 15.   Obligation to Participate in the Actual Operation of the Franchise Business
Item 16.   Restrictions on What the Franchisee May Sell
Item 17.   Renewal, Termination, Transfer and Dispute Resolution
Item 18.   Public Figures
Item 19.   Financial Performance Representations
Item 20.   Outlets and Franchisee Information
Item 21.   Financial Statements
Item 22.   Contracts
Item 23.   Receipt

There will also be a list of exhibits, usually listed by alphabet. They will include:

- Financial Statements
- The Franchise Agreement
- Licensing agreements
- Table of contents of the operations and training manuals
- List of franchisees
- List of franchisees who have left the system
- List of state administrators
- Agent for service of process
- State specific addenda to Franchise Disclosure Document (FDD)
- Other pertinent and relevant additional information

Perhaps the best way to prepare a list of questions is to prepare that list by item number.

Item 1 – the Franchisor, any Parents, Predecessors and Affiliates

You should read the section on the franchisor and its predecessors and affiliates closely. Read about the background of the business and the business experiences of its principal officers. Perform a search on the company and its previous officers. Plus, any information you can obtain regarding the record of the previous businesses – including other franchise businesses – with which the principles were associated, is very important. I have personally turned down consulting / employment opportunities based on this information alone after discovering some very unfavorable information. Do your research! This information alone can also help determine the possibility of your own success.

Questions to consider in item 1:

- How many key officers/principals are listed? How long have each been with the company? Where were they before their present job? Is this a one-person company? Or a corporation with a management team that is well trained and experienced?
- How many "layers" of the company are there? In the event of liability or error, what will your recourse be against the parent company? Is there a Franchise Sales division that is separate, or a subsidiary, of the actual franchise company? What is the liability of the broker you are dealing with in association with the franchise company?
- How many years has the franchisor been in actual operation of the products and services they are offering as a franchise? How many years have they been franchising this concept?

Item 2 – Business Experience

This section will give you some personal information on the officers and directors of the franchise company for the past five years. It should include the chief executive officer, chief operating officers, financial, franchise marketing and sales, training and support officers. Try to check out their backgrounds through conducting an Internet search, both their business experience with former employers, competitors and possibly, suppliers. You should make every attempt to get to know these people as much as you can. Ask to meet the CEO/President of the company before you make any down payment or deposit. Remember, these people will be crucial to your success, since their experience and expertise will directly affect you and your franchise business.

Questions for Item 2:

- Will I get to meet either in person, or by phone, the principals listed in Item 2? Will I get a chance to meet in person, or by phone: the site selection manager? The training manager? The start up trainer? The field support person for my territory?
- Do field consultants offer help and guidance or merely act in a regulatory role?
- Does the franchisor staff attend seminars on franchising and management?

Item 3 – Litigation

Pay close attention to this section of the FDD. Stay away from any prospective franchisor that is under some current injunction or restrictive order, particularly one that could result in a drastic change in the franchise operation, including possible cessation of the franchise. In addition, determine whether or not the franchisor, or any of the franchisor key employees, have ever been convicted of crimes or has an unfavorable record as determined by courts or government agencies. Again, conduct an Internet search on the company and the officers.

Franchising itself is a highly litigated industry. Simply having litigation listed in this section does not necessarily make it a bad thing. Some of the most mature and successful franchise brands have extensive litigation listed in this section. Pay close attention to determine if there is a recurring accusation and/or theme in the listing. For example, it would be considered unfavorable if a franchise was in operation less than five years and had several pending litigation accusing the franchisor of lack of support or possibly approving bad locations. However, if a very mature franchise operation had only four or five pending litigation for renewal issues, support issues or monetary claims from royalties and/or purchases, which would not necessarily be cause for alarm.

In my personal experience, sometimes a franchisee simply doesn't follow the system of the franchise. And when they go bankrupt, they refuse to accept responsibility for their own failures. That is, they want someone else to be accountable for their failure. And because of the amount of money involved, it is easy to sue someone. It may not even have anything to do with the franchisor's lack of support. So it is important to note what *types* of litigation the franchisor is involved in. Again however, if you see a recurring pattern, that should be reason for further research, or more questions for the franchise representative.

If no litigation is listed, consider that a good thing. However, that could be a result of not being a franchisor for long.

Questions to consider for Item 3:

- In how much litigation is the franchise involved? Franchising is a highly litigated industry. It is simply part of the industry.
- If there is only a small listing of cases in progress, or where decisions have been made, ask the franchise representative to explain those cases. And pay close attention to how he explains what the issue was about, and how it was resolved.

Item 4 – Bankruptcy

This section must disclose any bankruptcy in the last 10 years that involved "the franchisor, affiliates, its predecessor, officers, or general partners." Carefully examine this section that refers to prior bankruptcies. It's not uncommon for franchise founders to have started franchises in different businesses and failed in each of them. Each business failure could be subject to a bankruptcy, but the founder/principal may have walked away with millions of dollars that is not subject to the proceedings involving their corporate entity. Clearly, the ones who suffer the greatest were the franchisee who invested a great deal of money, only to see the value of their dream become worthless. Actually, it has been my experience that it is rare to find a bankruptcy under this section. Rare, but still possible.

Questions to consider for Item 4:

- If there is a bankruptcy listed in this section, ask the franchise representative to explain further.

Item 5 – Initial Franchise Fees

It should come as no surprise that if you are considering the purchase of a franchise, there will be a franchise fee. You can sort of think of it in terms of being very similar to a membership fee, or initiation fee, like you might pay a country club. But it is referred to as the franchise fee, or sometimes the initial franchise fee. In addition, you may be required to pay other types of upfront fees for certain services such as training, software, or point of sale systems. You will find the fees will be represented in table form, and quoted in a range from minimum to maximum. It is very important that you determine from this section precisely what you will receive in the way of services, inventory, and other benefits in return for those listed fees. If it is not stated what you receive in return for those fees, ask anyone you need to ask until you get a satisfactory answer. If you are considering more than one franchise brand in a specific industry, compare the upfront fees against other franchise brands in the same industry. Determine if they are similar or if there is any one brand that charges significantly more than the others. You will also want to ask current franchisees if they were satisfied with the benefits they received upon paying for these services.

In many cases, the initial franchise fee is a number basically picked out of the air. It should be a relevant number associated with the cost of opening the franchise. Some franchisors make money on the initial franchise fee. Others actually lose money on the initial franchise fee after the cost of getting your location open. You should ask the franchise representative how the initial franchise fee is determined (and how it is used). See if he can justify the initial franchise fee. A high initial franchise fee does not necessarily mean the franchise is a better investment or even a good one. In your research, expect to find a wide range of initial fees. However, there should be some uniformity of initial franchise fees within a particular industry. Be sure you were able to determine what the average is for a given industry.

Questions to consider for Item 5:

- Just be aware of what the INITIAL fees are, and for what services they cover and if they are refundable or not if you should decide not to pursue the franchise.
- Are the payments to the franchisor (or any affiliates) payable in installments?
- Are they to be paid before opening? Or when?
- What, specifically, do I receive in the way of services, inventory and/or other benefits for the Initial Franchise Fee?
- Is the amount of money required consistent with your available personal financial resources?
- How does this start-up money compare to starting and operating the business as an independent?

Item 6 – Other Fees

This section is also usually displayed in the form of a table. It will list any other fees that you will have to pay in addition to your initial franchise fee including: ongoing royalties, service fees, training fees, software and internet/web hosting fees, renewal fees, transfer fees, advertising fees and any other similar, one-time or ongoing charges and state to whom the fees are paid, whether it is payable to the franchisor, it's vendors or affiliates. Once again, check with the franchisor to determine if these fees are refundable if you choose not to pursue the purchase of the franchise (before) and after you have signed the Franchise Agreement. It is crucial that you determine how these amounts will affect your working capital and early projections in profit & loss from operating your business. You will need a good accountant. A good accountant is very valuable in assisting with the purchase of a franchise. See Chapter 7, "Questions You Should Ask Your Financial Advisor".

Some (most) franchisors require you to pay a royalty on gross sales. Remember that this percentage will be substantial in terms of the impact on your net profits. For example, 8% of gross sales could impact your bottom line after cost of product and overhead is taken into consideration. Again, you should certainly discuss what financial impact the royalty and other required fees and how they affect your income statement with your accountant (See Chapter 7). Also be aware of how the required fees will affect your pricing and how they compare to the fees of your competition in your local marketplace. It is a very good idea to consult with your accountant on how the fees affect your pricing and profits (Chapter 7). It is possible that the royalties and other fees could put you at a pricing disadvantage in your marketplace. However, the consumer also realizes that there are price/benefit trade-offs. You certainly need to be aware of these as well. The franchise representative *probably* will not be able to discuss this with you.

Questions to consider for Item 6:

- Are the fees payable only to the franchisor?
- Are the fees imposed and collected by the franchisor?
- Will the fees change, or increase, as my sales increase?
- What if my sales dip below a certain level? Do I still have to pay the fees?
- Is there a penalty for using a vendor outside the approved network? And what advantages are there to using an approved vendor in the network?
- Are the fees non-refundable or at least describe the circumstances when the fees are refundable.
- Whether the fees are uniformly imposed, i.e. do you have to pay the same advertising and marketing fees that a franchisee in a major metropolitan market pays if I am in a small market?
- Is the voting power of franchisor–owned outlets on any fees imposed by cooperatives? If franchisor–owned outlets have controlling voting power, disclose the maximum and minimum fees that may be imposed.
- Is the transfer fee negotiable? Can the buyer pay the transfer fee?

Item 7 – Initial Investment

This section will also be displayed in the form of a table. It will present the franchisor's estimate of what it will cost you to begin operations, including the initial franchise fee, equipment, inventory, rent, working capital and other miscellaneous costs. It must include both pre-opening expenses and those incurred during the initial phase, extending at least three months following the opening until the franchisee can break even (I have usually seen it stated for the first *year* of operation). You should pay very close attention to make sure that the amount has been adjusted to estimate the accurate cost for each particular state where the disclosure document is available. The information in Item 7 is crucial when trying to estimate how much of your money will go into the ramp-up, or start up of the business and how fast. Many of the items included in the estimate will be items you may already own, such as a computer, an automobile, perhaps a fax machine, and you can make them available to include them in the start up of the business. If you are going to use items you already own, make sure that those items pass the franchisor's standard in the operation of the business. The good news is you will not have to buy those items you already own. And you will not have to spend the money for those items that are listed in the Item 7 initial investment table.

Pay close attention to the amount of time that is stated for the ramp-up period. Some franchisors will only include a three-month start-up, and some others will realistically include a one-year start-up. You can interpret the ramp up/start up period by the amount of suggested working capital as stated in the table.

After your review of the FD it will be necessary to contact current franchisees and see if the cost projections were fairly accurate according to their experiences with their own start up. The questions to ask franchisees will not be included in this chapter. There is a separate Chapter 5 – "What Questions You Should Ask the Existing Franchisees". And the questions to ask pertaining to accuracy of stated start up costs are included there. If there are no current franchisees available, review the costs with local contractors and vendors to ensure that the costs represented in the table are an accurate and realistic financial projection. If the figures are significantly misrepresented, it is a violation of the law and you may need to report it at some future date.

You will notice that the total investment at the bottom of the table will be represented as a range. This range will, of course, will represent the lowest amount and the greatest amount necessary to invest in this franchise, and your total investment *should* be somewhere in between.

Also important at this point, compare the total costs listed in the table and compare your resources available to invest in this business. It is important that you do not spread your financial resources too thin! That is the wrong way to get your business started and is a recipe for disaster!

Questions to consider for Item 7:

- Do you realistically have enough money to make the total investment?
- Are the fees payable only to the franchisor?
- Are the fees imposed and collected by the franchisor?
- Are the fees non-refundable or at least describe the circumstances when the fees are refundable.
- Do you have to lease the premises from the franchisor?
- Do you have to buy/lease the furniture, fixtures and equipment (F, F &E) from the franchisor?
- Am I allowed to put an item that I already own (such as computer, fax or auto) into the operation of the business? Is it up to the franchisor's standards?
- Will I be allowed to put other applications on my computer that will help me run my business?

Item 8 – Restrictions on Sources of Products and Services

Pay close attention to Item 8. If the FDD states that franchisees must purchase or lease from specific sources, this should be a red flag for you to investigate the franchise further. If you are required to purchase or lease a particular product from the franchisor or their affiliates, you may be incurring excessive expenses as a result. Determine if the purchase contracts are competitive with unaffiliated suppliers, both in costs and benefits received. Legally, the franchisor must disclose if any officer of the company owns an interest in any supplier and whether a purchasing or distribution cooperative exists. Also, it is important to keep in mind that one of the benefits of buying a franchise in the first place is the advantage of group purchasing power. If there are designated, specific sources from which you must buy, then it should have advantageous benefits such as lower discount pricing, quicker delivery, free delivery, or smaller minimum purchases.

It is possible for a franchisor to set very low initial franchise fees and ongoing royalties to be very low. And then require the franchisee to purchase products exclusively from them. This could suddenly become a very expensive proposition, creating a competitive disadvantage in the marketplace and the investment in the entire franchise a very bad mistake. So, it would be very wise to check with existing franchisees (again, in Chapter 5) to see how they feel about the restrictions on being able to buy product from competitive sources to determine if they are getting a fair deal. What you should be looking for is a franchisor that spends most of their resources on licensing, training, promoting and operating a franchise business without being in the business of selling/leasing equipment, inventory and leasing facilities to franchisees. Are they a franchisor, or a financial services company? Always determine cost/benefit.

If you are required to buy products exclusively from the franchise or, it should be a proprietary product that your competitors are not able to buy for their business, also. Buying from your franchisor *should* give you a competitive advantage...not a competitive disadvantage!

If franchisors are able to lower the royalty fee by getting a portion of the profit they need from selling product or services to their franchisees at a reasonable cost, everyone benefits.

As with most franchise brands, you will be required to submit any advertising you wish to do to the home office for approval before placing the order. This is standard and actually benefits all franchise units to ensure that everyone is using the trademark and logos consistently.

Questions to consider for Item 8:

- Determine if required purchases from the franchisor are proprietary products that are not available anywhere else. If they are not proprietary products available exclusively from the franchisor, why are you being required to buy them exclusively from the franchisor?
- Does this arrangement create a competitive advantage or disadvantage?
- Determine if you're buying the same product with the same specifications at a competitive cost.
- Check with existing franchisees to see if they are happy with the required purchase contract.
- See if they are getting volume discounts, or contract pricing from outside vendors and suppliers based on negotiated arrangements from the home office.
- If you find a suitable vendor or supplier in your local market that can provide the same product, or close to it with comparable benefits, can you add them to the preferred vendor list? Or be allowed to buy locally?

Item 9 – Franchisee's Obligations

This is yet another item that is presented in the form of a table. Obviously, by the title, this section will list your contractual obligations as a franchisee. In the table, it will include references to the sections of your franchise agreement that include the listed obligations. The purpose of the table is to clearly summarize your primary obligations under the franchise agreement and any other agreements. The table makes it easy to help you find more detailed information about your obligations in these agreements as well as in other items of the FDD.

It is imperative that you read over the provisions of the agreements listed in this section very carefully. They clearly state your contractual obligations of the franchise agreement. If you are not able to comply with the terms and items listed in the table, it could very well be grounds for terminating your franchise. Make absolutely certain that you are willing and capable of complying with the obligations as listed.

It is important to study the quality of the franchisor's products and services and compare it with the competitor's product and services. If you find that the franchisor's products or services suffer in comparison, reconsider purchasing this franchise. I say this because many times it is difficult to comply with your provisions of the agreement when you do believe in the products and services. If you do not believe in the quality of the products and services, or not passionate about them, it is going to be even more difficult to comply.

Questions to consider for Item 9:

- Are your obligations and duties under the contract reasonable?

- Do all franchisees have the same obligations and duties?
- Are those obligations necessary to help ensure the uniformity and quality of the franchise brand, service or product?
- Is training required? Have all franchisees gone through the same training?
- Are there any provisions in the contract that requires what days the franchise must be open? Also the same for the hours of operation?

Item 10 – Financing

It is very rare to find a franchisor that will finance the purchase of the franchise. The fact that they might should be a red flag. Study the offer and take the offer to your local banker or financial advisor. Determine if the terms of the offer or comparable to what you can secure in the marketplace. Sometimes, an unethical franchisor will offer very advantageous terms to increase their franchise unit numbers. Also, consider that they might be your supplier as well. If they are selling more units in order to sell more product, which should also be a warning sign. Again, if this is an issue, check with existing franchisees.

It may be necessary to secure financing through the franchisor or else face the prospect of being unable to purchase the franchise. If it is a requirement to finance through the franchise door, visit with your local lender to determine whether or not you will be securing a loan on favorable conditions. Try to get a credit check on the franchisor. And again, check with existing franchisees to determine if financing through the franchisor has been a satisfactory experience.

If you will be seeking an SBA loan to finance the purchase of the franchise, the franchise will need to be listed on The Franchise

Registry. This is a searchable database of franchises whose Small Business Administration loan applications receive a streamlined review, from franchise information and analysis provider FRAN-Data and the SBA.

Dealing with banks and getting loans will be discussed further in chapter 7 – "Questions you should ask your Financial Advisor".

Questions to consider for Item 10:

- It is very unlikely, but it never hurts to ask; do they finance any part of the investment?
- If they finance, what has been their default rate?
- Will they help in preparing a loan package for commercial lenders? Or the SBA?
- Are they listed on the franchise registry?
- Get full details as to what the financing specifically covers. For example, the initial franchise fee, site acquisition, construction or remodeling, initial or replacement equipment or fixtures, opening or ongoing inventory or supplies, or other continuing expenses.
- The identity of each lender providing financing, especially such as leasing companies, and their relationship to the franchisor.
- Is the franchisor willing to guarantee any portion of the debt? Or guarantee a site lease?
- Can the debt be prepaid without penalty?

Item 11 – Franchisor's Assistance, Advertising, Computer Systems and Training

This section was formerly called "Franchisors Obligations". One would think that this particular section would be filled with many obligations from the franchisor. Because of the nature of the investment, including the franchise, the franchise fee, initial investment, total investment, one might conclude that this particular section, item 11, would include many obligations from the franchisor. However, this is not so. I have seen some franchise disclosure documents that actually stated:

"except as listed below we are not required to provide you with any assistance".

You're not only initially paying for the right to use a trademark or brand name; you are also paying a cash advance and a percentage of your future profits for other benefits to be provided to you by the franchisor. Make a list of the support items you believe are most important that the franchisor must provide to you in order for you to be successful. Compare your list to the statements in Item 10.

You should research the type of business thoroughly. Then determine what it would cost you to go into this business by yourself, without the franchise. Then compare the cost of the franchise to the cost of being an independent. The difference should be the number of benefits, support and training you get for the benefit of buying the franchise. What you will not be able to determine is the value of the non-tangible assets such as brand-name strength.

The most important obligations in *any* franchise offering should be:
- Access to operations manuals.
- Access to Training Manuals (if they are not the same).
- Site selection assistance.
- Initial and On-going Training.
- Opening inventory.
- Opening supplies.
- Grand opening assistance and advertising.

- Ongoing support from field support staff.
- Access to approved vendors and suppliers
- National Account / group purchasing power.
- Access to support staff to answer questions during office hours.

Once again, you should contact current franchisees and/or potential franchisees of a competitor/franchisor who can give you a good idea of what to look for in the way of training and support from the franchisor. Remember that each franchisee you contact also went through the same things that you are presently going through. A telephone call to an existing franchisee of the franchise operation you're interested in, or to a competitors franchisee, might give you the opportunity to meet the owner and discuss your needs. You can also get more information on contacting franchisees in chapter 5. (You will see a list of questions you should ask of existing franchisees regarding training, initial support and on-going support).

Questions to consider for Item 11:

- Does the franchisor state in the FDD that they will furnish a list of specifications vital to the operation of the business? Could you come up with the specifications on your own if you were to start your own independent business?
- Do they provide you with starting inventory, training, supplies and advertising?
- How long is the training, who teaches the classes, and where does training take place? How often is training conducted?
- Who pays for Training? Lodging, Transportation? Is it convenient?
- Is training taught from the Operation Manual?

- Is it possible to view the Operations Manual prior to signing the Franchise Agreement? (To determine the extent/scope of training).
- What ongoing support does the franchisor provide once the franchise is open and operating? (The Franchise Sales Representative should be able to give a good list).
- Is there adverting provided by the franchisor at the franchisor's expense?
- Are we contractually required to spend a certain percentage of our revenues for local advertising? Or is it just a recommended amount?
- How much in additional fees are required for advertising?
- Are the services being offered actually meet the franchisee's needs or is it merely "fluff" to look as if there is more support than what is really necessary or needed?
-
- Are the royalty payments reasonable for the level of support/service provided by the franchisor? (Ask existing franchisees this question, also – see Chapter 5).

Item 12 – Territory

The discussion of territory always seems to be more important to the prospective franchisee then it does to the franchisor. Let me explain. The discussion of territory is actually quite complicated. When the franchisor grants an "exclusive territory", it usually means that they will not sell another franchise in a designated/market/trade area within an identified radius/zip code/city, etc. Sometimes, in order to protect a given exclusive area that the franchisor has granted, they will require performance standards. They do not want to sell, or giveaway, an area for someone just to sit on it like "squatter's rights". Remember, that they are giving up something also. Also remember, that just because they will not sell another franchise unit in your area, that doesn't mean that a competitive franchise, or independent person, won't open a competitive business right across the street from you! You might want to consider which is better: a competitive unit with the same brand name (creating brand strength)? Or another competitor with a different name (who can steal your customers)? I hope you can see that the matter of exclusive areas can certainly cause problems for the franchisor. For instance, it should be discussed how a customer located in your area is being serviced by a franchisee in another area, or by the company-owned franchise unit. What about a customer who lives in your area and buys online?

There are usually restrictions on selling into another franchisee's area. Selling into an area might be restricted, but certainly calling on customers in another area most certainly would be restricted. That is, passive versus proactive selling into another area. The franchise system must be concerned because it realizes each franchisee must maximize their sales efforts to the maximum. Therefore, if one franchisee fails to develop their area to its full potential, it is quite possible, even probable that the franchisor will place another franchisee in competition in that area; this ensures that the franchise potential is fully achieved.

Most franchisors fear that a franchisee will not fully develop their territory, which is one reason why many franchisors will not grant exclusive areas. As mentioned earlier, some franchise agreements provide that the initial franchisee must meet current sales and/ or production minimums or risk losing the franchise, or having to share the territory with another franchisee. If this is the case, make sure that there are specific formulas for determining the size of the territory in order to have an adequate customer base to provide a reasonable profit to a franchise in each territory. Be sure to research the impact on your sales with such a condition.

It is highly unlikely that a franchisor will deliberately try to destroy an area by selling another franchise into a territory that would provide only a suitable profit for only one unit. If *two* franchisees fail, it looks bad for the brand's image and they will have to report it in their next FDD and it creates the potential for a lawsuit, which of course, no one wants. If they do not have a policy, or formula, which describes what criteria establishes a franchise unit location, then I would certainly not consider buying this franchise. Most franchisors have a formula to determine what justifies a location. Whether it is a certain number of homes in a radius, or number of business postal deliveries in an area/or ZIP Code, population, traffic, competitors, foot traffic, building permits, etc. Whatever it is, you should ask what the formula is.

In most cases, you will find that you are not being granted an exclusive area / territory. If not, find out if the franchisor will offer you a "right of first refusal" so you can purchase any additional franchises that may be offered in the future that might be adjacent to your specified territory or location. This way, you can expand in a given area without fear that someone else is going to open in your area, encroaching on your customers / profits. One benefit for you, as a prospective franchisee, is a condition set forth by the franchisor that they will not open any company-owned units in your territory under the same, similar, or different trademark / brand name. In large, mature franchise networks, it is very possible that they may retain the right to sell a franchised trademark product or similar product in your territory through supermarkets or other retail distribution channels. Think of Starbucks selling ground coffee and beans in grocery stores, with an actual franchised location across the street. It is possible that this could hurt your sales. The franchisor is required to disclose in the FDD any pre-existing rights of the franchisor, or another franchisee, to sell through other channels of distribution such as supermarkets, etc.

It is another whole subject to consider if the franchisor grants exclusive *account protection* in lieu of territory protection. An exact excerpt from another FDD states, *"Customers from whom you may solicit orders for Products and Services also may be restricted by means of account or other protections."* This means that you would be able to sell to anyone, anywhere as long as that account is not protected by another franchisee in the same system. But that also means that another franchisee can sell to an account in your general trade area, even if the account is located right next door and receives terrible service! The ruling goes both ways. This can be a very sticky subject. Just know what the rules and policies are before you sign the Franchise Agreement.

You should pay close attention to any termination, or loss of "area exclusivity" clauses imposed by the franchise or for failing to meet minimum sales requirements / quotas. Your franchise could be terminated if you do not meet these minimum sales volume quotas. If the franchise you are considering imposes such minimal restrictions, you should examine them carefully to see if they are realistic. Again, this is where it would be most beneficial to consult with existing franchisees to see what their experience has been at meeting minimum requirements (Chapter 5).

Questions to consider for Item 12:

- Is there an exclusive area agreement?
- What are the criteria to justify a location in any given trade/market area?
- If the area is large enough to justify more than one location, can I be given a right of first refusal if anyone else is interested in putting in another location?
- Am I required to maintain minimum performance standards to keep my franchise? And right of first refusal?
- To your knowledge, have any franchisees lost their fran-

chise for failure to meet minimum sales quotas? Or lost the right to renew for the same reason?

- Is the franchisor selling into my trade area through existing channels of distribution such as supermarkets? Or online sales?
- Is there account protection? If so, what are the rules pertaining to such?
- Does this company compete with the franchisees in the marketplace?

Item 13 – Trademarks

One of the main reasons people buy a franchise is for the well-known brand name, trade name, trademark, service mark or logo. It is required that the franchisor disclose in the FDD what the franchisee's rights are if the franchisee is required to modify or discontinue the use of the trademark under any circumstances.

You would want to be the licensee of a trademark or service mark that is registered in the United States Patent and Trademark Office (USPTO). A registered trademark or service mark gives the franchisor certain legal presumptions as to ownership and the right to use these marks throughout the United States, which is very valuable to your franchise. Remember, when you buy a franchise, it is a *license* to use the trademark or logo...you do not own it, you did not buy it. The franchisor owns the mark and can restrict how it is used. However, it is required that the FDD include a warning notice if the principal trademark is *not* registered with the USPTO.

Don't assume anything. Make it a point to check with the USPTO and find out if a certificate of registration has actually been granted to the franchise. The trademark registered in the Supplemental Register does not carry the same legal rights. A statement to this effect must be included in Item 13 of the FDD.

Take note of how long the franchisor has held the USPTO certificate of registration. An indication that the mark has been applied for, but is still pending, does not mean that the franchisor has, or will, attain the registered right to a particular name or trademark. Furthermore, the initials "TM" after the trademark only indicate that the franchisor uses a particular name as a trademark, not that the franchisor actually has a USPTO registration certificate.

The reason you will see "TM" after a trademark is that the key to protecting a trademark is to federally register it so the trademark or service mark can be used in advertising and using the symbol ® indicate that it is a US registered trademark. Actual registration of a trademark is only one component to consider.

Further consideration should also be given as to whether or not the franchisor is obligated to protect the trademark and pursue those who infringe on it. It not only benefits the franchisor, but the entire franchise system, to closely monitor and police the use of the trademark and immediately stop, or report, those who infringe on the mark no matter how petty or small, the violation, nor with any regard to the cost of the litigation.

Questions to consider for Item 13:

- Is the Trademark well known?
- Is it federally registered on the principal register at the US Patent and Trademark Office (USPTO)?
- Has it been use for a substantial amount of time?
- Are the trademarks and brand names well known in the market area in which I intend to open my franchise?
- Are they well known throughout the United States? If

not, what region has the strongest recognition?

- Is the trademark or brand name so well identified with the franchisor that it would attract customers to the operation?
- Will I have full use of every trademark, logo and brand name registered to the franchisor?
- Is there a section in the operations manual, or a separate manual, that fully explains the use of the logo in different applications? Such as a "Standards Manual" on the proper use of the name and service marks?
- Will you protect my rights to use the marks, or to protect me against claims of infringement or unfair competition?
- Are there any disputes pending or threatened against the trademark?

Item 14 – Patents, Copyrights and Proprietary Information

This section on patents and copyrights is important only if the patents and copyrights are crucial/material to the operation of the franchise business or service. If this is the case, request copies of the patents from the USPTO and have your patent attorney review them. Determine coverage and length of time remaining on the patent. Are there any possible limitations of the right of the franchisor to use the patent? Will there be any dissolution of the patent, through licenses to others, especially potential competitors? Pay close attention especially to any claims of proprietary right and confidential information designated by the franchisor.

Usually, the only copyright protected items is normally in a computer system, including software, manuals, customer lists, pricing information, sales aids, correspondence and communication with suppliers and vendors, training, advertising and promotional materials, and other written materials relating to the operation of the business.

This information is usually treated as trade secrets and you must treat any of this information confidentially. You and your employees must agree not to communicate or use confidential information for the benefit of anyone else during and after the term of the franchise agreement. This confidentiality is usually secured in the form of The Franchise Agreement, a confidentiality agreement or employee agreement.

It is unusual for a franchise to own a *proprietary* patent or trademark that is crucial, or material, to the operation of the business. Again, this section is important only if that is the case.

Questions to consider for Item 14:

- Are there any patents or copyrights that are crucial/material to the operation of the business? If so, what is the length of time remaining on the patent?
- Is there any litigation in any court affecting the use of the copyrights?

Item 15 – Obligation to Participate in the Actual Operation of the Franchise Business

If you are researching a franchise to be an absentee owner, this section will be of interest to you. Some franchisors prohibit absentee ownership, even if you hire a competent manger because it skews the financial model of the franchise. This section pertains to whether the franchisee must personally participate in the actual day-to-day operation of the franchise. If there is no such requirement, this section must state whether the franchisor recommends such participation, whether the manager must complete the franchisor's training program and/or own an equity interest in the franchise entity, and any limitations that the franchise must place on its manager.

I have been employed in a couple of franchise brands in which it is an absolute requirement that the franchisee *must* participate in the operation of the franchise. Both of these franchises were both B2B models in which the business was built with the necessity of sales calls being an integral part of the business. It was more of an accountability issue. In larger franchises such as a hotel, or retail operations, this would not be as big of an issue.

In many franchises, it is believed that the successful franchisee is the one who manages their own business, or at least spends considerable time supervising the management of the business. As stated in the previous paragraph, in most cases, the franchisor will contractually require, or at a minimum, at least *insist* that the franchisee retain a qualified manager to run the business. In most cases, the manager will need to actually be approved by the franchisor, and be obligated attend the training program, usually at the franchisee's expense.

The following example is direct from an actual Item 15 in an actual FDD, (brand name withheld):

"Our current policy is to require the Franchise Agreement be initially signed by an individual franchisee. If the franchisee properly forms a business entity to hold the Franchise which is wholly--owned by the franchisee, we will permit the franchisee to assign the Franchise Agreement to that entity in accordance with the Franchise Agreement. If you are an individual, you must personally direct the operation of your ABC-XYZ Business. If you are a corporation, limited liability company or other business entity, you must identify an individual that we approve to personally direct the operation of your ABC-XYZ Business ("Principal Owner"), and all owners must sign a guarantee of performance. The entity must at all times be at least 51% owned by the Principal Owner. You may, at your option, designate a manager to supervise the operation your

ABC-XYZ Business; provided, that you and your Principal Owner will remain fully responsible for the manager's performance. If you choose to appoint a manager to assist you in the operation of the ABC-XYZ Business, that manager must be approved by us and attend and successfully complete the initial training program. Your managers, employees, and agents must sign confidentiality/non-compete agreements in the form required by us."

If you plan to actually participate in the daily operation of your franchise, this is not as big of an issue to you. Absentee ownership is another issue. Read this section closely.

Questions for consideration on Item 15:

- Will I be required to personally participate in the operation of the franchise?
- What if I delegate the management to my wife or children?
- Is the training program good enough to make the manager proficient in the operation of the business in my absence?
- What about in the event of long-term illness, or incapacitation?

Item 16 – Restrictions on What the Franchise May Sell

If you wish to grow your business by offering more than the core franchise offering of products and services, you may wish to pay close attention to this section. It would normally be prohibited by the franchisor to offer additional products and/or services that are outside of the core business of the franchise brand.

This is especially true of a small franchisee that would offer the spouse's hand-made handicrafts over in the corner of the front of the business. Or if the franchise is a B2B model, offering window-tinting or food products. There have been many instances where the franchisee was limited to one-service *only*. For example, it would be prohibited for a franchisee that owns a tire store franchise to grow their business by offering compatible services, such as tune-ups, or brake replacement.

In a franchise brand, the key word to remember above all is "consistency". The franchisor wants *all* locations to offer the same product and services so that when a customer seeks the same franchise brand in another city, the buying/shopping/dining experience is the same in all locations. This is the basic premise of franchise ownership. Consider if the situation was reversed. That is you run your franchise "by the book" and another fellow franchisee of the same brand was selling something in his location that you thought was unprofessional, or was looked upon as lower standard. It affects *all* locations. If you were hoping to sell additional products/services, your concern should be whether or not such restrictions on your product sales will allow you to make a reasonable profit.

Questions to consider for Item 16:

- Can I get permission to sell additional *compatible* products and services in my franchise?
- Are fundraising products also restricted, such as Girl Scout Cookies? Or local raffle tickets?
- Are there any restrictions to account protection, as to *whom* I can sell products and services?

Item 17 – Renewal, Termination, Transfer and Dispute Resolution

Again, another very important section of the FDD. You may be getting an idea by now of the importance of the FDD document.

It contains so much vitally important information that you should absolutely be aware of before you enter into such a long-term, mostly restrictive, agreement. It might be appropriate at this point as a reminder again, that it is not only important to pay attention to what information the FDD contains, but the information that it *doesn't* contain! And again, that is the purpose of this book...to help you basically "dissect" the FDD, section-by-section.

Item 17 is also presented in table form. It is of such major importance to your franchise success, since it states the length of time for which you will receive a return on your franchise investment. Ideally, the best franchise is one in which, as long as the Franchise Agreement has not been breached, the franchise will exist (and be renewed) for as long as the franchisee(s), their heirs, or their purchasers perform the duties as contracted by the terms of the Franchise Agreement. Of course, the Franchise Agreement is for a designated term, or period of time. But as long as the agreement remains beneficial to both parties, franchisee and franchisor, you would want to feel secure that the Franchise Agreement will be renewed. A Franchise Agreement that requires you to spend 10 or 20 years of your time, money and effort only to lose the franchise at the end of the period is not a good investment. There are unethical franchisors that have shorter-term agreements that they do not renew (or make it difficult to renew) and they churn owners to get additional franchise fees. It is *always* imperative to talk to existing franchisees (Chapter 5). Tips on talking to existing franchisees will be found in the next chapter.

The FDD requires that the Franchisor explain what "renewal" means for the system and, if applicable, a notice that the franchisee may be required to sign a different contract/agreement with different terms and conditions.

Beware of clauses that will require you to make significant "upgrades", repairs, decorations and remodeling as a condition of re-newal. Some clauses are reasonable requiring the franchisee to invest in a "re-branding" or "new look", but will contain a formula so that the expense will not have to be incurred short-term, or less than a year. And in many of those cases, the franchisor will offer an allowance for those upgrades. The clause define some type of standard so that any changes in furniture, windows, paint, furnishings and fixtures (and sometimes, equipment) are related to staying competitive and "fresh" within an industry.

Almost every franchise has a Transfer Fee. What you will want to notice is if the transfer fee is reasonable. Of course, 'reasonable' can be a relative term. An ideal franchise is one that you can pass on to your heirs or sell to others (subject to the approval of the Franchisor) at a reasonable fee. Having been on the Franchisor side of the transfer, please also be aware that there is a lot of work by the franchisor to make the transfer. Most transfer fees are in the $15,000 - $30,000 range. That would be a 'reasonable' fee. Usually, the buyer, or heirs, would pay the fee either direct to the Franchisor, or in the purchase price of the business being transferred. If the Franchisor does not allow such transfers or renewals, and you still wish to purchase the franchise, consider what provisions, if any, you can make for the franchisor to purchase the franchise back from you and at what amount of consideration for the purchase.

A good franchise will allow you to change forms of business type (from sole proprietor to LLC, for example) without incurring an extra fee, or at least a minimum fee.

Pay very close attention to the reasons a franchisor gives for causes of termination when reviewing this section of the FDD.

Notice if the franchise is *allowed* to be offered for resale. In many cases, the franchisor may have the right of first refusal. Make sure that this transfer does not include passing the business on to an heir, or blood relative. Basically, the more rights you receive regarding the continuation of the franchise, as well as the transfer and sale of the business, the better franchise you are receiving, at least from a legal point of view. Also, since the amount of the transfer fee is defined in the Franchise Agreement itself, by the time you are ready to sell you franchise, the amount of the fee may actually be viewed as a more affordable amount.

There are many forms of contract resolution. Among them are litigation, arbitration and mediation. And then there are varieties within each. There are one, two and three member arbitration boards and/or panels. There is binding arbitration and non-binding arbitration. If the franchise agreement limits your choice to arbitration rather than a court of law, or your choice of the law to be applied is an out-of-state jurisdiction, consult an attorney regarding the effect of this on your legal rights. Without exception, in every franchise agreement I have ever seen, disputes between the franchisee and franchisor, and the relationship between you and the franchisor will be governed and construed under and in accordance with the internal laws of the state in which the franchisor headquarters is located. Of course, you should consult a franchise attorney regarding the effect of this on your future rights. There are more questions you should ask your franchise attorney in chapter 6.

Questions you should consider for Item 17:

- Under what conditions would my franchise not be renewed? Is renewal generally assumed as long as my franchise is in good standing and I have met all the conditions of fulfilling the franchise agreement?

- Under what conditions would my franchise be terminated? With or without cause?
- Under what conditions can I terminate the agreement?
- Under what conditions would a sale of franchise not be approved?
- Do I have to offer the franchise for sale to the franchisor as a right of first refusal first?
- Can you share with me the conditions of the last five or ten terminations?
- How much is the transfer fee?
- Is there a non-compete provision post termination? Is there a non-compete provision post transfer or sale? For how long? And how far from the place of business?

Item 18 – Public Figures

This section of the FDD requires that the franchisor disclose whether it uses a famous person to endorse the franchise and/or products and services. If so, it must disclose the compensation paid or promised to the person, the person's involvement in management or control of the franchisor, and the amount of the persons investment in the franchise brand.

Questions to consider for Item 18:

- If the franchisor is paying a public figure to endorse the franchise, find out whether or not you can use the person (or their likeness) in personal appearances or in advertising without prior written approval of the franchisor, how frequently you could do so, and the cost of such use, if any.

Item 19 – Financial Performance Representations

First, please understand that there are entire books written on Item 19 by itself alone. It is without a doubt, the most debated, contested and written-about section of the FDD. There are blogs, websites, books and magazine articles written about whether a franchise should (or should NOT) include an Item 19 Financial Performance Representation (FPR) in their FDD.

The franchise industry is a highly regulated industry by many agencies of the federal, state and local government. The main federal regulator for the franchise industry is the Federal Trade Commission (FTC). Here is a direct excerpt from a very recent actual FDD:

"The FTC's Franchise Rule permits a franchisor to provide information about the actual or potential financial performance of its franchised and/or franchisor-owned outlets, if there is a reasonable basis for the information, and the information is included in the disclosure document. Financial performance information that differs from that included in Item 19 may be given only if: (1) a franchisor provides the actual records of an existing outlet you are considering buying; or (2) a franchisor supplements the information provided in this Item 19, for example, by providing information about performance at a particular location or under particular circumstances.

We do not make any representations about a franchisee's future financial performance or the past financial performance of company-owned or franchised outlets. We also do not authorize our employees or representatives to make any such representations either orally or in writing."

This is pretty standard. In my 25+ years of franchise experience, I have never been employed by a franchise brand that included an Item 19 FPR. I cannot stress enough in this section how greatly Item 19 is debated in the franchise industry. There are as many franchisors and franchise attorneys who want to see inclusion of an FPR as there that contest that the numbers can be manipulated and do not represent reliable earnings projections. And the debate continues...

With all of that being said, this is the *main* reason I have chosen to write this book. Because after someone makes an initial inquiry to the franchise, an initial phone interview is scheduled. The franchise sales representative will be completely prepared. Usually, the initial interview is a scheduled phone call that will take about 40 minutes to an hour to complete. The franchise sales representative will have all of their questions prepared. They will have a questionnaire that will list all of the questions to which they will need answers.

During the course of the hour-long interview, the sales representative will ask you many questions. They will learn a lot about you. They will know your work history/experience over the last 10 years, your skill set, management experience, how much money is in your 401(k), how much money you have in the bank (checking and savings) and the amount of equity in your home(s). They will want to know what your credit looks like, what your monthly living expenses are, when (and where) your children will be going to college. They will want to know the same details for your spouse and/or significant other. They will also want to know what your hobbies are, what do you like to do for fun. They will also want to know what you liked about your last job (and what you didn't like about it, also).

Of course, they will want to know what your goals are. Why do you want to change jobs? Why do you want to buy a franchise? Why that particular brand?

In short, they will discover a lot about you and your family. They will be fully and completely prepared with their questionnaire and list of questions.

At the end of the interview, you will feel exhausted. You will feel as if you have just been interrogated. Then, they will ask you what questions you have for them. And of course, the most logical question you will have, will be, "How much money can I make?" And if the franchise is one of the 65% of those franchises that do not have an FPR in their Item 19, their reply will be, "Well, I sure wish I could share this with you, BUT franchising is highly regulated by the FTC. By law, I cannot disclose that information to you. But after you have reviewed the FDD, I can show you and tell you how to get the information from our existing franchise network. Do you have anymore questions for me?" And from my personal experience, your reply probably will be, "No".

Unfortunately, in the thousands of interviews in which I have participated, this is how the initial interview plays out. The franchisor has all the information he needs about you and you have nothing, or very little. I have heard many frustrated prospective franchise buyers over the phone; you can hear the disappointment in their voice. Now, they have to make the first decision as to whether to move forward with very little information or give up the process completely, giving up on what was previously thought to be their hopes and dreams. The most dangerous option is to move forward, buy the franchise with inadequate answers and insufficient research.

In most cases, as stated, the franchisor usually will not provide an FPR because federal and state laws requiring written substantiation of such projections. If the franchisee fails to meet the projections, it would represent grounds for misrepresentation and of course, litigation.

If the franchise you are interested in, and are investigating, actually provides an FPR in their item 19, you should first show it to your accountant for their evaluation. (Again, see Chapter 7). Then compare it with the information you receive from talking to existing franchisees. And still yet, also compare it with franchisees (and independent) competitors. You *must* feel confident that the FPR you have been presented is reliable and accurate. Also, you should be aware of market differences. One can be profitable in a small market with half the sales revenue of a unit in a large, more costly, market.

Also, if the franchisor makes an FPR to prospective franchisees, the franchisor must have a reasonable basis and written substantiation for the representation at the time the representation is made and must state the representation in the Item 19 disclosure. They must also disclose the following:

a) Whether the representation is a historic financial performance representation about the franchise systems existing outlets, or a subset of those outlets, for is a forecast of the prospective franchisees future financial performance.

b) If the representation relates to past performance of the franchise systems existing outlets, the material bases for the representation, including:

  1) Whether the representation relates to the performance of all the franchise system's existing outlets or only to a subset of those outlets that share a particular set of characteristics (for example, geographic location, type of location, such as freestanding versus shopping center, degree of competition, length of time the outlets have operated, services or goods sold, services supplied by the franchisor, and whether the outlets are franchised or franchisor-owned or operated.

  2) The dates when the reported level of financial performance was achieved.

3) The total number of outlets that existed in the relevant period and, if different, the number of outlets that had the described characteristics.

4) The number of outlets with the described characteristics whose actual financial performance data were used in arriving at the representation.

5) Of those outlets whose data were used in arriving at the representation, the number and percent that actually retained or surpassed the stated results.

6) Characteristics of the included outlets, such as those characteristics noted in paragraph b1 in this section above, that may differ materially from those of the outlet/unit that may be offered to a prospective franchisee.

c) If the representation is a forecast of future financial performance, state the material bases and assumptions on which the projection is based. The material assumptions underlying a forecast include significant factors upon which a franchisee's future results are expected to depend. These factors include, for example, economic our market conditions that are basic tool franchisees operation, and encompass matters affecting, among other things, hey franchisees sales, the cost of goods or services sold, and operating expenses.

d) A clear and conspicuous admonition that a new franchisee's individual financial results may differ from the results stated in the FPR.

e) A statement that written substantiation for the financial performance representation will be made available to the prospective franchisee upon reasonable request.

If a franchisor wishes to disclose only the actual operating results for a *specific* unit being offered for sale, it need not comply with this section, provided the information is given *only* to the potential purchasers of *that specific* unit.

If a franchisor includes an FPR, it may give you a feeling of complacency. You might not thoroughly investigate the validity of the numbers and go blindly on the numbers they have given you. You could make a very expensive mistake in relying on those numbers. However, if no FPR is made, I can show you how to get very reliable numbers in chapters 5 and 7 of this book...probably even more reliable than if there were an FPR present. There *is a way* to get good reliable numbers...with, or without an FPR in Item 19.

Be aware that a franchisor cannot suggest that you call certain franchisees, *unless you specifically request it on the grounds of similar background, geography and/or other demographics.* They cannot simply "steer" you to the most profitable franchisees in order for you to get positive feedback.

Questions to consider for Item 19:

IF an FPR is represented:

- Can you explain the basis and substantiation on which the FPR is based?
- In *your mind,* what is the single most important thing I should be looking at in this Item 19?
- What percent of franchisees are hitting those numbers? Can this be substantiated?
- What if I do everything you ask me to do in my first two years, and I don't hit those numbers?
- Is there any adjustment for more expensive markets with higher overheads?
- (to yourself) Will you be able to replace your existing salary on what the FPR shows? Will you need to buy more than one unit to maintain your present standard of living?

IF an FPR is **NOT** represented:

- How do you suggest that I get reliable financial information without the FPR in Item 19?
- Can you suggest franchisees for me to call based on my background? My geography?
- What is the success rate of existing franchises?
- What method is used to protect franchisees from poorly performing franchises?
- How many franchisees should I call to get a reliable idea of financial performance?
- What do you suggest that I ask them to get the information I need?

NOTE: In the next chapter (Chapter 5), there are many ideas on *how* to talk to the existing franchisees to get the information you need. These questions above are questions you should ask the *franchisor* after review of the FDD.

Item 20 – Outlets and Franchisee Information

This is also (another) very important section and will be a valuable source for you to attain additional information not stated in the FDD. This section provides you with the names, telephone numbers, and locations of existing franchisees. It is a roster of their current franchisees. In addition to accessing this information, you can also determine whether or not a substantial number of failures have occurred within the franchise operation in which you are investigating. You can also project future growth of the system in a few years, according to the estimates of the franchisor. Not very reliable estimates, but you get a feel for their desired direction.

Normally, the more mature the franchise system and the greater number of franchisees, the greater the franchisor's chances for success and future sales of franchises. We have all heard the axiom, "Success breeds success". This is especially true in the franchise industry, when each year, there is a "Flavor of the month" aka:"franchise of the year"...where more franchise sales begets more franchise sales. However, this is not always true. *Always* check with existing franchisees. It is also an unwritten rule that the more franchisees, the higher the franchise fee and the more you will pay for the franchise. This is especially true in situations where the franchisor does not have many company–owned units. In theory, a greater number of franchised locations indicate a more extensive market penetration of the franchise brand and product or service and a more positive public image for the franchise.

You will always get the best and most realistic information about your future franchisor from the existing franchisees. (Next, in chapter 5) If there have been a significant percentage of franchise terminations, cancellations, or non—renewals, let this be a warning and you should proceed with caution.

You will also want to discuss the turnover rate with the franchisor. The turnover rate is the percentage of franchisees that close their business in a given time period. Item 20 will give you this data, state-by-state for the three years prior to the current year. You will also find contact information for some franchisees that closed their franchise within the past year. However, franchisors are allowed to select which franchisees they want to offer for this item, and it is good business for them to choose those whose experience has been positive. Following is an example of how a business closing can be positive:

- A franchisee wanted a short-term business for his or her retirement.
- The franchise was bought for a son or daughter, and was sold for a profit.
- The franchisee retired from the system.
- The franchise was sold at a significant profit.
- The franchisee had a good experience, but was ready to leave for another opportunity.
- The franchise was successful, but the franchisee wanted to leave for health, family reasons or other reasons unrelated to the business.

On a personal note, the franchise my parents owned only for a short period of time was sold for a significant profit after only two years because someone made us an offer we couldn't refuse! We were the only location in a very high growth of area of the city, and the new owner really wanted the franchise badly, recognizing the potential growth. Guess what? He was right! He more than tripled the business over the next few years as the city grew in that direction...everyone was a winner!

If you see a table of projected openings that includes your state in which you want to open your franchise, do not be alarmed. However, you should at least ask your franchise representative to explain if there is a *probability* of that unit opening and where it is located. If the location listed in the table is merely a "blue sky" projection that is okay. With that being said, also pay close attention to the table that lists terminations and see if there are any in your state. You should ask the franchise representative to explain the circumstances around that termination (or non-renewal)

As suggested in the next chapter, *always* be sure to call as many current and former franchisees as you can and ask the questions as stated in the next chapter.

Questions to consider for Item 20:

- Determine if there are projected openings in your state and ask the franchise representative to explain.
- Determine if there have been terminations in your state and ask the franchise representative to explain.
- Are there any company–owned units for sale in the state in which you wish to open?
- If any company-owned units come up for sale, can I be given a first right of refusal?
- If a location is being terminated close to my market area, how are those customers communicated to? Can we be given a chance to service those customers? (Especially if the franchise is a B2B / service franchise).
- Do they have very little turnover of franchisees in their system? How many franchisees have left the system? Do you ever see locations that have closed down? Why? Do they have a roster full of long-term franchisees?

Item 21 – Financial Statements

The FDD will contain an exhibit with audited financial statements. You should certainly take the financial statements to your accountant if you do not have the proper training to evaluate them. You will want to know that the franchisor is a viable, successful operation that can sustain their future. If not, they can leave you holding empty promises.

As I have seen personally, most franchisors will use a separate corporate entity for selling franchises. However, if the franchise in which you are investigating doesn't, you then have an opportunity to find out whether or not these company-owned ventures actually made an income for a period of up to three years. It would be good to know that if you are going to be following their system, that they are able to make a profit. If they can't, can you?

Be aware that the financial statements are the financial position and track record of the franchisor, (not the franchisees). As stated above, you should ask your accountant to analyze the financial statements. Have them analyze, evaluate and list any questions that you should bring to the attention of the franchise representative. If you require the services of a an accountant, be sure that they are familiar with the FDD document and how a franchise operates.

Questions to consider for Item 21:

- Unless you are adequately trained to do so for yourself, have your accountant list questions for you that he sees as a problem area in which you should be concerned. (See Chapter 7)
- You should also determine if these are the financial statements of the franchisor, or their parent company. The franchise operations may represent only a very small fraction of the total operation.
- Clearly, what you are looking for is financial health and longevity.

Item 22 – Contracts

This section requires the franchisor to attach a copy of *all* form contracts the franchisees will sign, including:
- the franchise agreement,
- Any license agreements (for software /computer use),
- Asset purchase agreements (if a resale),
- Equipment leases,
- Premises leases,

- Purchasing contracts/agreements,
- Options
- General release

I cannot stress enough that if you have an attorney review the franchise agreement, please make sure that it is a *franchise* attorney. They understand that a franchisor will not be willing to alter the franchise agreement. If you hire a regular, general attorney, you will be wasting money because you will pay him to review an agreement and make suggestions that cannot be implemented. The franchise agreement is not negotiable. This is for consistency in the system. What a franchisor does for one franchisee, he must do for the other (under the terms of the FDD in use at that time). Simply stated, if you cannot live with the terms of the franchise agreement, do not buy the franchise.

Again, this is merely a listing of all the forms/agreements you will be required to sign. As you will see in chapter 6, questions you should ask your franchise attorney, the questions relative to The Franchise Agreement will be discussed in that chapter.

Questions to consider for Item 22:

- Do they have a fair franchise agreement? As mentioned previously, the system is in the operations manual. But that system is enforced through the franchise agreement. It would appear that's the franchise agreement strongly favors the franchisor. It just needs to be fair to allow you to renew the agreement as many times as you wish, and transfer your franchise easily and fairly without (excessive) transfer fees. Probably the most important issue is allowing you to sell the equity in the business when the time is right.

- If you must lease the premises or equipment from the franchisor, is it a fair lease? Can you secure the terms of the lease on your own with another firm? Are the terms of the lease in line with what other landlords and/or leasing companies are offering?

Item 23 – Receipt

In this final section of the FDD, the franchisor is required to include as the last two pages of the FDD, a form for the prospective franchisee to sign that acknowledges receipt of the FDD. Whether you proceed with this franchise or not, you are still required to sign the receipt and send one copy back to the franchisor.

Please note: By signing the Receipt page, you are simply stating that you have *received the disclosure document on a certain date*. Nothing more. There is nothing binding in the acknowledgement of the receipt. Sign it and return it if you wish to proceed. This is normal procedure.

Questions to consider: none.

In your research, you may hear or see the term "Uniform Franchise Offering Circular" (UFOC). The FTC created the UFOC to protect the buyer from unethical franchisors. When the FTC changed the standards and requirements of the period of time that a prospect has to be disclosed before any money can change hands, the document name was changed to the Franchise Disclosure Document FDD. Which is what is in use today. Again, it is to give the prospect as much information as possible to make an informed decision about the considered franchise. It is a useful tool, but not the end-all final source. It contains a lot of information. But there is a lot of information that it does *not* contain.

Is the franchisor willing to answer *all* of your questions before you buy? Certain legal restrictions can prevent a franchisor from answering some of the questions (such as "how much money can I make?"), but all the others should be answered satisfactorily. The most useful information comes form the existing franchisees...in the next chapter.

CHAPTER 5

Questions You Should Ask the Franchisees

"If one advances confidently in the direction of his dreams,
and endeavors to live the life which he had imagined,
he will meet with a success unexpected in common hours."
—Henry David Thoreau

OK. You're still with me this far. Great! You have made the initial inquiry, gone through the initial interview, reviewed the FDD and had a FDD follow-up call. And you're still interested in getting to the next step...which would be to talk to the existing franchisees. The due diligence phase. At this point, you now will be investigating the franchise on information *other than* what the franchisor has told you. In the franchise sales process, this step is *crucial* to conducting your due diligence. In talking to the existing franchisees, you will learn significantly more than what you have learned from the initial interview from the franchise development/sales representative and reading the FDD. I think talking to franchisees is where the rubber hits the road, so to speak. After your discussions with franchisees is where you will decide to move forward, or not.

It has always amazed me how much research one will conduct before buying a television, or a bed or some electronic gadget. But when it comes to pushing a significant amount of money to the middle of the table to buy a franchise, one will go blindly forward without talking to any existing franchisees, or just a few. I just don't get it.

This stage of the process is what is referred to as the *validation* phase. Where you validate everything that you have read and have been told with the people who are actually on the front lines doing it, the ones who have pushed their money to the middle of the table and living their dream (or nightmare).

These are the people who have already gone through what you are now going through. They have met with the franchise sales representative; they have reviewed the FDD, talked to their financial advisor and their legal advisor, and still made the decision to move forward. They have been through training, signed the Franchise Agreement and are running their franchise, for better or worse. They intuitively know what mistakes they made and what they would go back and change, if they could. You can learn from their mistakes...and their success. You definitely want to hear their point of view. What better advice can you get than from those who have already walked in your shoes?

It is also important to point out that just because they have decided to move forward and become franchisees, not everyone makes a decision for the same reason. We all have different reasons for motivation. We all have different passions in life, different monetary goals, and resources with which to work. It's not a one-size-fits-all proposition.

For example, you may discover in your talks with franchisees that one franchisee is disappointed because he is only generating $150,000 per year in profit, while you may be perfectly comfortable with generating $100,000 per year. Referring back to the very first chapter of this book, it is important to know what your goals are. Then, design your questions for existing franchisees so that you will know how best to invest in a franchise that will help you achieve those goals.

Two things are very important when being directed by the franchise sales representative to talk with existing franchisees. 1) Do not let them suggest which franchisees you should talk to. If for any other reason besides having a similar background as you, geography, or similar-type location, it is illegal. It is called *steering* and is prohibited. As you probably have guessed, if it were up to them as to which franchisees you should talk to, they would want you to talk to only the most successful ones. 2) They should be willing to direct you to "talk to as many franchisees as you possibly can" or "any and all existing franchisees". Period. Not three, not five...not ten. To *as many as possible.*

It is possible on your very first call, you may talk to a franchisee that is not successful. Or it is possible they are just simply having a bad day. So, if you talk to the first two or three franchisees who are not doing well, or all having bad days, you could quickly form the opinion that this would not be a worthwhile investment. But then, as you go along, the next three are "raving fans" about the franchisor, are making good money, and are very happy with their investment. And so, in this scenario, you have now spoken to six franchisees and have a 50-50 result. It would certainly dictate that you would call at least another ten.

If it is a new franchise that doesn't have many locations yet, call every franchisee that is on the roster. Then, call as many competitive franchisees as you possibly can. You don't want to be somebody's guinea pig at your expense!

Being Prepared

Pay close attention here. I cannot stress this enough: Being courteous and gracious will get you *much more* information that being intrusive and rude. You want crucial information, right? Well, you don't call these very busy business owners out of the blue and ask them (read: interrogate them) about their business and how much money they make. Would *you* be so accommodating? So, when you get the roster, call ahead (preferably during a non-busy time), introduce yourself, state why you are calling and make an appointment (phone or in-person) to ask them "just 10-15 questions and take no more than 15 minutes of their valuable time". Seriously, only ask for no more than 15 minutes, and they will most likely be gracious enough to give you an hour, if they get to pick the time slot for you to call (or visit). But do not ask for more than 15 minutes. And let them choose when it would be convenient to have the discussion. They really are very busy people.

Then... BE PREPARED! Have your questions written down. You certainly do not want to hang up, or leave, and wish you had asked questions that you didn't think of. And of course, I think it goes without saying that if you make an appointment to talk to an existing franchisee, you better not miss it or be late!

Don't Be Surprised If

Don't be surprised if they do not want to be so accommodating. They may not even want to talk to you! They may view you as a competitor, or future competitor. In my personal experience, I have heard so many existing franchisees say that they are all for network expansion, but "not in my backyard!" So, they may not be willing to talk, they may try to discourage you. You should probably talk to franchisees that are outside of your market area (or where you plan to open your location). So, look at the roster to find out-of-town locations (or do an on-line search). The franchisee in your local market area might find you threatening. This is especially true if they are new themselves and are still trying to get to breakeven. And even more true if they are *not* new and are still struggling. Be prepared to hear anything and everything... good and bad!

With the above being said, do not fear making contact...it MUST be done!

The List of Questions

The following is a somewhat exhaustive list. You *cannot* ask every question to *any* franchisee. This list is prepared to give you an idea of some of the important questions I have heard over many years' experience. Find 10-15 to which you want answers and consistently ask the same questions to get an idea of the range of answers. *Do not* print out the list and send it to the franchisee. It is too overwhelming...and you are asking them to do your due diligence for you.

Be sure to write their answers down and gauge the responses on what their expectations for the franchise were before starting out. If you can determine that their expectations were unrealistic, put their expressed dissatisfaction in perspective (and compare to your own expectations as well).

- *Why* did you buy the franchise? What were your expectations for your franchise?
- How long have you owned your franchise? Was it a start-up? Or resale?
- Was the training adequate? Did it actually prepare you for the reality of running the business?
- Are the Operations Manuals helpful?

- Is the franchisor easy to work with?
- What support did you receive between when you signed the Franchise Agreement and when you opened? And since you opened?
- Do they help you on an on-going basis?
- What was the most valuable help the franchisor gave you during start-up?
- Is the field support staff knowledgeable and helpful?
- Do you feel that the Operations staff / headquarters staff are qualified, knowledgeable and competent to solve most problems over the phone when you call? Are they responsive?
- Is there continuing training and development to support your continued growth?
- What has been the greatest challenge in owning your franchise? What has been the easiest aspect of operating your franchise? Any "pleasant (or unpleasant) surprises"?
- What do you like the most about owning this franchise? And what do you like the least?
- What are the competitor franchises? What are your thoughts about them?
- Are you making a profit? Is your income above or below what you expected?
- What are your average monthly sales now? What were your first year monthly sales?
- Did you make a profit in your first year?
- How is cash flow?
- How many employees do I need starting out?
- IF there was an Item 19 Financial Performance Representation (FPR) in the FDD, was it representative of actual income expectations? ***See footnote***
- Are you comfortable with the amount of debt you are carrying?
- Are you on track to meet your financial goals?

- How did you get realistic earnings expectations before deciding to buy your franchise?
- How long did it take you to hit breakeven? How long before you saw a return on your investment?
- Did the franchisor accurately project the start-up costs (and total costs) in the FDD? Any suggestions on how I can do better?
- Is the franchisor's advertising effective? Do you feel that you get any benefits from it? Are you happy with it?
- Are you happy with the promotions and marketing done on your behalf by the franchisor?
- When you experience a problem, how responsive is the franchisor? Do they actually resolve the issue?
- What problems or issues have you had with the franchisor?
- Are they too restrictive? Demanding? Or pretty much let you mange how you see fit for your business/marketplace?
- Are they honest and fair?
- Do you have an owner's council or advisory board? Have they been helpful?
- Are you reasonably satisfied with the Franchise Agreement?
- Have you had any disputes with the franchisor? Were they reasonable to deal with during the dispute?
- Was there any legal action by you or the franchisor?
- Do they actively listen to your problems and concerns?
- Is there effective communication between the franchisor and the franchisee?
- Is the quality of products and services from the franchisor consistently high?
- Are there any issues with any other franchisees? How was it resolved?
- Do you know some of the other franchisees? Anyone in

particular who I should contact? Or not contact?

- How would you rate the helpfulness and communication between fellow franchisees?
- Are you happy with the contracted / authorized suppliers? Are the prices and service comparable to what else is available from other competitive sources?
- How much are you required to buy directly form the franchisor? Is it comparable to what I can buy elsewhere?
- Are your products and services uniquely competitive? How so?
- Have you heard of any trouble with franchisees renewing their Franchise Agreement?
- Have you heard of any franchisees having trouble with selling and/or transferring their franchise?
- To your knowledge, have any franchisees ever been terminated without just cause?
- Is there anything the franchisor doesn't provide, but you wish they did?
- Are you generally satisfied with your relationship with the franchisor?
- How selective are they in awarding franchises? The quality of franchisees in a system can affect the overall quality of that system. This will also give you an idea of the focus of the franchisor. Are they just selling franchises to anyone? Or are they concerned about a consistent experience in each market place? The value of your investment is also determined by the experience the ultimate customer has from each franchisee.
- As you talk to several of the existing franchisees, compare yourself with the most successful (and least successful) franchisees in that system and ask yourself which one(s) you most closely resemble.

And the single, silver bullet question of all...
* *Knowing what you know now, if you had it to do all over again, would you buy this franchise again? If so, what would you change?*

The answer to this single, important question will tell you their level of overall satisfaction. If you only had time to ask one question, this should be it. However, it doesn't answer *all* of your concerns. You still need to know "why" or "why not". It is a great question with which to wrap up the interview.

Don't ignore their responses, comments or concerns, positive or negative. Take good notes and determine answer differences between them and yourself. As stated earlier, everyone does different things for different reasons. We are all different...we have different goals, passions, likes and dislikes. Perhaps you might have stronger experience, or a more diverse background...perhaps they have more financial resources on which to rely. These factors can have a huge effect and can make a <u>great</u> difference in one's chances of success.

It could be extremely helpful if you could possibly locate any *former* franchisees of the specific franchise brand in which you are interested. There, you will be able to get excellent information from such a primary resource. Just remember, that if any particular franchisee has been terminated, or lost his franchise, they could be very bitter about their loss. If you are talking to a former franchisee, try to determine the circumstances for their departure from the system. But regardless, you might want to listen *compassionately* to their impressions and opinions of the franchisor. This person may be in financial ruin. If there are too many former franchisees, consider this to be a red flag regarding the purchase of a franchise from this particular franchisor. Obviously, a high number of failures by previous franchisees are a <u>*major*</u> red flag!

Buy A Franchise With Confidence Using these 4 Questions

By Dr. John P. Hayes

Some prospective franchisees admit they do not know what to ask existing franchisees, and others say they know what they'd like to ask, but they don't know how. Don't let either scenario stop you from thoroughly investigating a franchise opportunity. Here are 4+ questions to ask, worded in a way to help you get the information you need.

#1 "As an existing franchisee, knowing what you now know, would you buy this same franchise again?"

Some experts will tell you never to ask Yes/No questions, but in this case you must because you want a definitive answer. If you ask ten franchisees of the same brand that same question you want to add up the "yeses" and "no's" at the end of your interrogation and decide if this is a franchise you should buy. If the majority of existing franchisees tell you "no" then you probably need to look for another opportunity. There could be exceptions, but you'll want to understand what they are before you go ahead.

The answers to Question #1 logically lead to other questions. Whether the franchisee says yes or no, ask: "Why" If the franchisee answers no, ask "Under what circumstances would you change your answer to a yes?"

The answers to Question #1 logically lead to other questions. Whether the franchisee says yes or no, ask: "Why" If the franchisee answers no, ask "Under what circumstances would you change your answer to a yes?"

#2 "Do you find the business as satisfying today as you did when you first got started?"

Satisfaction is an important consideration in the life of a franchisee. In fact, many people explore franchise opportunities to get away from an unsatisfying job. But in this case, you'll pay a fee to go to work. Do you really want to work at something that you don't find satisfying after a year or two?

It's another Yes/No question, but again the answers lead to other questions: "What happened to change your degree of satisfaction?" . . . "What could you or the franchisor do to make the business more satisfying?"

#3 "What's the secret to the success of the top franchisees?"

It's an open-ended question that can reveal important facts for you to consider. For example, if the franchisee answers, "Location!" you need to zero in on where to open your franchise. If the answer is "sales skills" or "management skills" or "accounting skills" you need to evaluate your own skills, or your ability to hire those skills.

Of course, if <u>you're not questioning a top franchisee</u>, you may get the wrong answer! That's why you should always ask the franchisor to give you a list of the top performing franchisees, i.e. the franchisees who won awards at the last three annual conventions. (A franchisor that won't do that or can't do that may not be worthy of your consideration).

#4 "If I invest the money the way the franchisor suggests (i.e. in training, advertising, location, etc.) and I work the business as well as you have, how much money can I expect to earn my first year as a franchisee? The third year? The fifth year?"

That's what you really want to know, isn't it? "How much money will I make?" The franchisor probably won't tell you, but the franchisees will if you ask in a non-invasive manner. If you're expecting to earn six figures annually, but no franchisee ever has with this brand, you need to know that upfront. It may mean you'll have to buy more than one unit to meet your financial goals.

While these are some of the questions you should ask existing franchisees, you'll find more in my book 101 Questions to Ask Before You Invest in a Franchise.

Dr. John P. Hayes is an author and speaker who specializes in franchising. He's one of the few people in the world who has been a franchisor, a franchisee, and an advisor to franchisees. His books about franchising are best-sellers at Amazon.com.

CHAPTER 6

Questions you should ask your franchise attorney

"Diligence is the mother of good luck"
—Benjamin Franklin

Now that you have decided to take the next step toward the idea of purchasing a franchise and have selected one or more possible franchise systems to operate, you should meet with a franchise attorney to discuss the offering(s) in detail. The main issue with franchising for most prospective franchisees is that they don't know what they don't know. Franchising is a complex – and heavily regulated – industry that requires prospects to not only proceed with caution, but also protect themselves by doing the required homework. In this chapter, we will discuss the critical questions to ask your franchise attorney, including questioning the registration process, the FDD itself and your ability to negotiate certain terms. As with many business ventures, knowing the best questions to ask is half the battle.

The first question you should ask your franchise attorney is: **Was I properly disclosed with a legally compliant FDD?** Your franchise attorney will be able to discuss the applicable laws and regulations in detail, but you should know that the franchise industry is regulated by the Federal Trade Commission's Rule on Franchising (the "FTC Rule") and also regulated by a number of state laws. The FTC Rule is why you have a giant stack of paper in front of you that explains the franchise you are thinking about buying. The FTC Rule requires franchisors to disclose certain aspects of their business and business experience in a 23-item document – the Franchise Disclosure Document (often referred to as an "FDD"). While the FDD may be daunting, it is important to read through it carefully and discuss certain parts of it with your franchise attorney.

Before we get to specific parts of the FDD, you should also know that the FTC requires the franchisor to disclose you with the FDD and then wait fourteen calendar days before taking money from you or signing a franchise agreement. Also, as stated above, several states have their own franchise registration laws, some of which have different waiting period requirements. There are also states that have relationship laws – laws that don't govern disclosure but govern certain aspects of the franchise relationship, such as termination. Ask your franchise attorney about the states with franchise laws, especially if you live in or will be operating your franchise in one of them. If you will be, one important question to ask your franchise attorney is: **Was the FDD registered with the state on the day you were provided with it?** You should also ask your franchise attorney for additional information about laws and regulations in the state where you live and the state where you are planning to operate a franchise (if different).

Regardless of what state you are in, **you should also consider in what month you were disclosed**. The FTC requires franchisors to amend their FDD annually, within 120 days of their fiscal year. A typical fiscal year ends on December 31, meaning the deadline for renewal would be April 30. If you were given an FDD in March, it might be wise to wait until the annual renewal version in April before you move forward. You also want to make sure that the FDD contains the most up-to-date financials, which also might be a reason to wait for the renewal version. However, you should discuss this issue in more detail with your franchise attorney, who can explain the reasons to wait (or not).

The second category of questions you should discuss with your franchise attorney revolves around: **How can I use the FDD to evaluate the pros and cons of the franchise?** As you read in Chapter 5, you should look for the contact information of current and former franchisees in an exhibit to the FDD and contact them. You should also ask your franchise attorney for questions to ask the franchisees. This way, you can be sure you are asking the right questions and getting the best picture of the franchise from those who work with the franchisor. As comprehensive as the FDD might seem, existing franchisees know the ins and outs of the business and how the franchisor treated them and can give a fresh perspective on the franchise system.

One of the most frequent franchisee questions is: **How much is this going to cost me?** Ask your franchise attorney to go over the initial fees, other fees, and the estimated initial investment – each of which has their own item in the FDD. First, the initial fees: These are the fees that you must pay to the franchisor (or an affiliate) before your franchise opens. The most obvious initial fee is the franchise fee, which you will pay to the franchisor in exchange for the right to use the system and its trademarks. In most cases, the franchise fee is paid in a lump sum and is non-refundable. You should also ask your franchise attorney to discuss the possibility of owning multiple franchises. Owning multiple franchises is usually covered by a development agreement, which likely provides for a discounted franchise fee if you purchase multiple franchises at the same time. If you are financially capable and otherwise willing to own and operate multiple stores, ask your franchise attorney to compare the development agreement with the franchise agreement.

Besides the initial franchise fee, other initial fees may include grand opening advertising, training fees, or manual fees. Be sure to discuss the types of fees the franchisor requires with your franchise attorney so that you understand which of the initial fees are refundable (if any), when each fee is due, and what each fee covers.

In addition to **initial fees, which are paid before the franchise opens**, there are also several other financial burdens that come with a buying a franchise. In a separate section of the FDD, the franchisor has to disclose all other fees the franchisee must pay to the franchisor (or its affiliates) or that the franchisor (or its affiliates) imposes or collects for a third party. **Other fees are required to be paid at some point during the franchise relationship** and include fees such as the royalty payment, advertising fees, renewal fees, transfer fees, computer software fees, and training fees, among others. Ask your franchise attorney to review these fees and when they are due, so that you can understand all of the fees you will be required to pay over the term of your franchise agreement. Once you have information regarding all of the fees, you can start to figure out the full picture (positives and negatives) of owning a franchise.

Perhaps the biggest piece determining whether you have the financial capability to operate the franchise is the **estimated initial investment**. In another section of the FDD, the franchisor has to disclose estimates for every cost you may encounter in order to open the franchise and also operate it for an initial period (at least three months). Ask your franchise attorney to review and explain the estimated initial investment with you and give his or her opinion on whether these estimates are reasonable. If you are only purchasing one franchise, then the estimated initial investment will cover all initial costs for that one location. If you are purchasing more than one location (via a development agreement) then the initial investment should give some idea as to how much it will cost to open each location. Ask yourself if you are financially capable of paying for all of these estimated costs. If you are planning on operating more than one store, also ask yourself if you are relying on the success of the first location to fund the second (or third).

Now that you know the costs of the franchise, you are probably wondering: **How much money will I make?** While not required, a franchisor may choose to include financial performance information in its FDD and may do so as long as there is a reasonable basis for the information. Ask your franchise attorney to review the financial performance representations as well as the included disclaimers to make sure that the information is worthy of your reliance. It is important to look for outlets that may have been excluded and the reasons for the exclusion. Does it seem fishy that the only stores included were in a particular area? Or, were all of the presented locations open for a significant period of time? It is important to realize that, as a new franchisee, you are not likely to make as much money as a franchisee that has been open and operating for several years. Ask your franchise attorney to explain what information is missing from the franchisor's FDD that is typically included in others, such as average gross sales, costs of goods, payroll expenses, rent, inventory, utilities, etc. Also, discuss with your franchise attorney any financial performance information the franchisor provided during the interview process or any informal meetings that don't match the financial performance information in the FDD, if applicable. Providing financial performance information that is not included in the FDD (except for a few limited exceptions) is a big red flag and you should ask your franchise attorney about the consequences of these actions, which are likely forbidden by the FTC.

Additional parts of the FDD that are worthwhile to discuss with your franchise attorney are the **litigation and bankruptcy his-**

tory of the franchisor and its officers. The FTC Rule requires franchisors to disclose certain litigation that is relevant to the franchise process as well as bankruptcy information involving the franchisor company and its management. Has the franchisor been sued by several franchisees for fraud? Has it paid large settlement amounts to disgruntled franchisees? Has the company, its CEO, President or other high-ranking management filed for bankruptcy recently? These are all questions to discuss with your franchise attorney, who can also provide some advice on how this information may (or may not) affect your success as a franchisee.

As you learned from reviewing the initial and other fees, the franchisor may be collecting money directly from you through the payment of fees. But, you should also know that **franchisors often collect money indirectly from you** (via rebate arrangements with vendors off of purchases you make) **and also directly from you** (via the franchisor or its affiliates selling products or services directly to franchisees). In the FDD, the franchisor is required to disclose all revenue earned from required purchases made by franchisees. Ask your franchise attorney to discuss these revenue streams with you and also how the franchisor uses the money. Does the money go back into the system? Is the franchisor keeping all of it as profit? Does the franchisor make most of its money from purchases made by franchisees? If so, the franchisor may be less focused on the success of the franchisees and more concerned with simply bringing franchisees into the system.

Importantly, when you become a franchisee, the **franchisor will license to you its trademark** to be used in connection with the business. The trademark is how customers will recognize your brand. Since the trademark will be such a large part of your business, it is important to understand everything about it. Ask your franchise attorney to review the trademarks and explain to you the advantages of the franchisor having a federally registered trademark and the disadvantages of an unregistered trademark. Ask your franchise attorney to research the trademark(s) to see if the franchisor is keeping up with all of the paperwork that is required to maintain the registration(s). Also, look in the FDD and on the Internet for any competitive uses of the trademark out in the world – are there non-franchisees trading off the trademark without the franchisor's permission? What has the franchisor done about this? Since the trademark is so important to the business, the franchisor should make an effort to stop known infringers. Ask your franchise attorney to explain how infringers near your area may affect your business.

Lastly, ask your franchise attorney to review the **relevant industry laws** that are included in the FDD. Does the franchisor provide only a general overview of laws or does the franchisor get down to the nitty gritty of local laws? Does it seem like you will have to fight through a lot of red tape to open your business? Ask your franchise attorney to explain any industry-specific laws that may affect your business, such as health or sanitation laws in the food industry or licensing requirements in child care businesses. It is also important to understand whose burden it is to investigate applicable laws. Is it yours? If so, it's best to ask your franchise attorney about them now, before you invest, so that you understand any restrictions these industry-specific laws may impose on your business.

Now that you have reviewed and discussed with your franchise attorney the above critical points of the franchise system, it is important to compare these terms with other franchise models. **Ask your franchise attorney to pull FDDs from competitors so that you can compare the offerings side-by-side**. FDDs are public information and a few registration states post FDDs on their website. This comparison will help you get a picture of the types of fees and costs other similar franchisors are imposing on their franchisees. You can also ask your franchise attorney to review and compare the financial performance representations regarding the competitor's franchisees. This comparison will help you determine how successful other brands are in your area. Besides financial information, ask your franchise attorney to go over with you the locations of the competitor's franchisees. If the competitors have an overwhelming presence in your market, it would be helpful to know that before you secure a location for your franchise.

After you understand the FDD and its parts, the next question to ask your franchise attorney is: **What are some of the critical deal points and which should I try to negotiate?** Whether or not the franchisor will negotiate will vary on a case-by-case basis. Ask your franchise attorney if he or she has ever dealt with the franchise system you are considering and see if the deal terms were negotiated. In general, the more established the franchise system, the less likely they will be to negotiate. Up-and-coming franchise systems might have more wiggle room because they are trying to build the system and grow their list of franchisees. Franchisors that have a dense network of franchisees will be more concerned with keeping all franchisees on the same page, rather than striking a deal with you. It is important to note that a franchisor being unwilling to negotiate doesn't necessarily mean that you should run away from the deal. In a franchise system with hundreds or thousands of franchisees, the franchisor is likely genuinely concerned with protecting the system and the goodwill it has established throughout the years. Generally speaking, if you become a franchisee, you would want all other franchisees to be bound by the same rules as you are. For example, you wouldn't want your neighbor franchisee to commit an act that damages the goodwill of the system and then have the franchisor unable to terminate that bad-egg franchisee because of a negotiated change in the franchise agreement. However, that being said, it is at least worthwhile to ask the questions up front and open the possibility of negotiation, instead of automatically taking the deal as it stands.

Now that you have decided to negotiate, which terms should you focus on? One area to consider is **renewal rights and renewal conditions**. If you are looking to invest in a long-term business, which you likely are, review the term of the franchise agreement and the renewal terms. Some franchisors don't allow for renewal, some only allow for one renewal term, and some allow for perpetual renewals. If there is only one renewal, perhaps consider asking for a second or asking for a longer renewal term. At the same time, also ask your franchise attorney to discuss the renewal conditions with you. These conditions will determine if you will be able to renew the franchise agreement for another term. Some common renewal conditions include, but are not limited to: (i) upgrading the store/fixtures/equipment, etc., as applicable; (ii) attending refreshing training; (iii) paying a renewal fee; and (iv) signing a new franchise agreement. It is important to discuss with your franchise attorney the renewal conditions so that you can get a better picture of what you will be faced with at the end of your term, especially those that may require a large capital expenditure. Most importantly, ask your franchise attorney about whether you will have to sign a new franchise agreement that may contain materially different terms than your current franchise agreement. After reviewing the list of renewal conditions, ask your franchise attorney which one(s) he or she recommends trying to negotiate with the franchisor.

In addition to renewal terms and conditions, another area to consider negotiating is the **reserved territorial rights**. Usually, franchisees are granted a specific geographical area (e.g. a county) in which the franchisor will not establish corporate outlets or allow other franchisees to open an outlet. However, some franchisees are not granted exclusive territories and, as such, may face competition from franchisees within the same system. Make sure to ask your franchise attorney to explain what rights the franchisor has reserved, particularly if within your territory. Are they allowed to establish a competing business right next door to you? Can they sell franchise-related products on the Internet to customers in your territory? These are just some examples of what franchisors may reserve the right to do, which may affect your ability to turn a profit in your area. It is important to discuss the reserved rights with your franchise attorney and ask where he or she thinks the franchisor may be flexible.

Another avenue to consider, regarding negotiation, is **whether the franchisor has negotiated with other franchisees**. How will you know? If you happen to be in California, ask your franchise attorney to review the California Department of Business Oversight's website for negotiated changes filed by the franchisor. In California (and only California) franchisors are required to disclose (to California-based franchisees) in the FDD and file with the state any terms different from those contained in the franchisor's FDD that have been negotiated with franchisees in California during the previous year. The purpose of disclosing the negotiated changes is to help control favoritism among franchisees by showing future prospects what other franchisees have been able to bargain for and then negotiate for those same terms or others. This disclosure is also helpful for those franchisees that are unsure whether the franchisor is willing to negotiate at all – by providing proof that the franchisor has done so in the past. However, if you happen to be in one of the 49 states that don't require the franchisor to disclose negotiated changes, then you will have to rely on the advice of your franchise attorney and possibly calls with existing franchisees regarding whether the franchisor will be open to negotiation.

Even if the franchisor is willing to negotiate, there are several terms that the franchisor is likely to stand firm on, which means you should fully understand each of them. **First, the term** of the franchise agreement or the development agreement. Most franchisors are likely unwilling to change the term in an effort to keep the system on a manageable (and predictable) timetable. However, in a development agreement, the franchisor may be willing to negotiate the development schedule. A development schedule dictates when you must open each of the outlets and sometimes are overly optimistic. It might be worth stretching out the schedule in an effort to make it more likely that you will actually be able to open the required number of stores. Review the timelines closely and think about the costs and effort it will take to open each store – then ask if the development schedule seems attainable. Also, ask your franchise attorney to explain what may happen to your business if you break the development schedule.

Second, provisions regarding the **territory and its exclusivity** or non-exclusivity are likely staying put. Ask your franchise attorney to explain the differences between the types of territories and what the franchisor may or may not do within or near your territory. As stated above, franchisees are typically granted a specific geographic area in which the franchisor will not operate an outlet or allow another franchisee to operate another outlet. A common issue to look for is when the franchisor may put "non-traditional sites" within your territory, such as kiosks at airports or smaller locations within sports arenas. It is important to discuss with your franchise attorney whether the franchisor is contracting a right for itself to put these types of locations within your territory and also discuss what ramifications these sites may have on your business. If you are planning to open in a college town where most of your business will come from students, then a franchisor's kiosk on that campus (a.k.a. a non-traditional site) might heavily affect your customer base. Discussing these possibilities with your franchise attorney will help paint a better picture of what your business will face as competition.

Third, **non-competition covenants** are generally very important to franchisors because they don't want former franchisees to compete with the franchise system by using everything franchisees learned as franchisees. For this reason, among others, franchisors are unlikely to negotiate a non-competition agreement, with the exception of perhaps limiting the scope (as opposed to removing it altogether). Ask your franchise attorney about your state's laws and how they might affect non-competition agreements. Some states, such as California and North Dakota, will not enforce non--competition agreements and other states will enforce them so long as they are reasonable. Make sure to fully review the non--competition restrictions with your franchise attorney and discuss how local law may or may not affect these restrictions.

Fourth, an important part of the franchise agreement is the section that discusses **termination**. For what reasons may your franchise be terminated? For the most part, franchisors are unwilling to budge on certain defaults and will not remove them from the list of reasons to terminate you, but may be more willing to add or extend a period to cure a particular default. Ask your franchise attorney if the list of defaults, especially those that do not provide for a cure period, are reasonable and if there are any he or she recommends should have a cure period (or a longer cure period). Defaults such a bankruptcy, criminal involvement and unauthorized transfers are common in the franchise world, so make sure the ones the franchisor are including in your agreement are common and fair to franchisees. Importantly, ask your franchise attorney to explain any cross-default provisions. These are provisions allowing the franchisor to terminate your franchise agreement if you breach another agreement with the franchisor. These provisions often arise in the case of development agreements – where you are signing more than one franchise agreement. For example, say you agree to open three locations and will have to sign three franchise agreements. What happens if you open one store, but fail to open the next store within the required time period? Does the franchisor have the right to terminate only the second agreement or the first one also? Ask your franchise attorney to explain this risk and make sure you fully understand how, when, and why the franchisor may shut you down.

Fifth, another important and often non-negotiable element of a franchise agreement is whether you will be required to sign a **personal guaranty**. A personal guaranty is used when the franchisee is a business entity and not an individual. While we are on the subject, you should ask your franchise attorney to explain the differences between signing a franchise agreement as an individual or a business entity. If you will be signing the franchise agreement under a company you have created for that purpose, the franchisor may then require you to sign a personal guaranty that then puts you on the hook personally for the franchisee's obligations. Further, the franchisor may also require your spouse to sign a personal guaranty. Ask your franchise attorney to fully explain the risks of signing a personal guaranty and what the personal guaranty requires of you. You will want to know if you are personally liable for future lost royalties in the event of a default, among other concerns. Your franchise attorney will be able to review the personal guaranty and shed light on the obligations it creates.

Lastly, **franchisors generally will choose a law to govern the franchise agreement, the method of dispute resolution and the location for any future disputes**. The governing law and venue may or may not be your home state. Ask your franchise attorney to discuss these provisions with you so that you understand where you will be required to take your disputes and which state's law will decide the issue. If your franchise will be located in, for example, New York, but the location of all disputes must be handled in Arizona, travel costs will need to be considered. In addition to the applicable law and location of a dispute, also ask your franchise attorney to explain what type of dispute resolution the franchisor has chosen. Franchisors may choose an internal dispute resolution, arbitration, mediation, litigation or some combination. Each avenue has advantages and disadvantages, so make sure you ask your franchise attorney about the dispute resolution choice in your franchise agreement.

Once you have reviewed all of the above (which is not an exhaustive list) with your franchise attorney and taken some time to digest the potentially overwhelming amount of information, it's time to take the franchise offering to the next business professional – your financial advisor.

*****

Fisher Zucker LLC is a full-service law firm with a national practice dedicated almost exclusively to franchise, distribution and licensing matters. The firm has offices in Pennsylvania and New Jersey.

Lane Fisher is admitted to practice in Pennsylvania and New Jersey and serves on the franchise law committee of the New Jersey State Bar Association, the Philadelphia Bar Association and the American Bar Association's forum committee on franchising. In addition to chairing its membership committee since 2005, Lane serves as a member of the International Franchise Association's Board of Directors and is a past member of its executive committee and a past chair of the executive committee of the Supplier Forum Advisory Board. Lane also is a former chair of the Legal Symposium Task Force and serves on the FranPAC advisory board.

CHAPTER 7

Questions You Should Ask Your CPA/Financial Advisor

Rule #1: Never lose money. Rule #2: Never forget rule #1
—Warren Buffet

The purpose of this chapter is to give you a quick overview of the financial part of the decision to purchase a franchise. If you've come this far you already have a desire to do whatever it is the franchise offers, care for old people, make pizza or whatever the business model is that you are now excited about doing yourself.

However, in order to get to that point you first have to come up with the money to be able to pay the franchise fee, buy the assets, do the tenant improvements and ultimately swing open the doors (so to speak) on your new venture.

In order to do that, you will need to access the capital necessary to complete the transaction, set up the business, run the business and support you and your family until the business actually makes a profit! No easy task.

Do you have a written business plan?

There is this ugly little "worst kept" secret in the business community. It's a statistic that has been around a long time and remains true even today. Pay attention:

Roughly 70 to 80% of all new business startups fail in the first eight years.

That means that if you're buying and starting a new franchise, according to statistics you have a one in five chance of making it. Now it's very important to note that there are certain franchise networks that significantly beat that statistic due to the training, education, support before start up and competency of the field staff that help you get to profitability.

Does your network provide field staff?

A reasonable ratio is approximately 30 franchisees for every field staff. If the network you're considering does not provide field staff support directly in the field, at least on a monthly basis to you, find another franchise.

What does a business plan needs to contain?

We believe that business owners have a plan, safely stored away in their head. The critically important step of getting that plan on paper in a format that is clear, and provides all the needed information for a business or financing partner to make a positive decision is absolutely critical to the success of the venture. Every competent business plan needs to cover the following topics with both a brief outline and substantiating data that backs up the narrative. The topics are as follows:

- Corporate data
- Description of the business
- Operational information
  Product
  Employment
  Sources of supply
  Management
  Marketing and distribution
  Competition
  Facilities
  References
- Financial information
  Historical (three years of P/L and Balance Sheets)
  Pro forma projecting a full year cycle
  Cash flow
  Personal financials of the principles
  Salaries and benefits
  Current outstanding debt

When these topics are covered and laid out in this order you have a business plan that can also be utilized as a loan proposal to seek the

Are you actually reading (not just skimming) the documents?

As you are contemplating buying a franchise, you will be inundated with documents for you to review and understand. The single most important will be the Franchise Disclosure Document (FDD). Understanding this document, the information that it provides, and the information that it does *not* provide, is critically important to your future success. Section 2 of this chapter lays out a series of questions that we encourage you to ask your financial advisors about the information you receive in the FDD. This is your own "due diligence" on the company that you are considering partnering with for your long-term future. These questions are critically important, but even more so are the answers.

What you can you afford to pay for your franchise and where will you get the funds?

There are really only four sources of money to start or grow a business. They begin with your personal **net worth** and the cash that you bring to the table. Next is the **trade credit** that you can receive from the vendors that will be working with you to set up your business and grow your ongoing operations. Third are the **retained earnings** that you will derive out of your business, which in a growing business, are never enough to fund your growth. Finally, you have the **bank,** leasing companies, credit card companies and all other financing sources that provide you capital, which you have to pay back. Sometimes, if your financing with your business with personal credit cards, at exorbitantly high interest.

Do you have enough Working Capital?

Working capital has many definitions, but the one that's most important for you is: "Current Assets (the assets that you can convert to cash in one year) minus your Current Liabilities (the bills you have to pay in one year) equals the money left over to run the business. In virtually every new startup business, the working capital that is set aside to fund and sustain the business is usually not enough to get the business to profitability. A good rule of thumb is to determine what you'll think you'll need and then double it. You should be good to go.

Will you have enough *Living Capital*?

This is an often gut wrenching assessment of what your family will actually need to live on for the first 12 months that you are running your new business. Do not, under any circumstances, expect the business to fund your lifestyle in the first year. If it turns out that it does, consider yourself highly lucky and a person that has beaten the odds, which as a new business start up, are stacked against you.

Once again, determine what you think you will need in living capital for the first 12 months of your new business operation and add at least 50% more to it, as a cushion. Adding the pressure of an underfunded family to a new business start up causes a level of personal and business stress that is one of the most common reasons for divorce among new business owners.

What options for business structure?

There are certainly tax benefits to business ownership, and I will be covering those as we review the various business structures that are available for you to establish your new company.

1. Sole Proprietor

This is the simplest yet most risky way to set up a business, and is the least preferred method to organize your new franchise business. It maximizes your personal risk, as you have unlimited liability for everything! This can include all the obligations that the business will incur, including things like your operating costs or possible judgments that could come as a result of legal action against your business.

On the positive side you also own personally all the assets of the business, including such things as your Accounts Receivable, inventory, all of your equipment and/or tenant improvements, as well as your real estate. In general, it is not recommended that you would own any real estate utilized by the business, as part of the business. It should be owned personally by you, but separate and apart from the business entity. Speaking bluntly, this is not the way to set up your new franchise.

2. Partnership

It's highly likely that you may want to go into business with someone else. As we say in Profit Mastery, "In the typical business there is usually someone that knows how to 'make it', and someone that knows how to 'sell it'. When the two of you get together, sometimes great things can happen. However, it is not a good idea to set up your franchise in any of the types of partnerships available, including general, limited and limited liability partnerships. Instead, utilize one of the corporate structures to help minimize your personal liability.

3. S Corp

The great thing about any of the Corporation forms of ownership is that, in general, they provide the owner with limited liability, as the business is a separate legal entity from its owners. A corporation must have a Board of Directors, establish minutes, hold annual meetings, and in general conform to the requirements of being a corporation. Sometimes in the world of small business this can be exceedingly challenging to accomplish.

In the most basic of terms, an S Corporation is a legal entity that is organized to be able to pass corporate income, losses, deductions, and credit through to the shareholders, specifically for federal tax purposes. Prior to the establishment of the limited liability company form of corporate organization, companies that previously had been run as partnerships or sole proprietorship's, were converted to S CORP.'s to take advantage of the limited liability benefits often utilized the S CORP.

In general, S corps are taxed very similar to partnerships; in other words, the income, deductions, and tax credits of an S corporation go directly to the shareholders. This avoids the double taxation of having the income tax both at the corporate level and the shareholder level.

4. C Corp

For a variety of reasons, including the issue of double taxation, C corps have fallen out of favor as the business organization entity of choice for most new franchisees. If you set up your new business as a C Corp and you are lucky enough in the first year to generate a $50,000 taxable income, you're going to pay a minimum of $7500 +25%. And you're going to pay personal taxes on any distributions that come to you as well.

5. Limited Liability Company (LLC)

This is the recommended organizational entity of choice, especially for a new business just starting up. For most new franchisees, the LLC or private limited liability company is the way to go. This structure combines the pass-through taxation of a partnership or sole proprietorship with the extremely important limited liability of the Corporation. It is important to note that a LLC is not a corporation; it is however a legal form of a company that provides limited liability to its owners. In general, this is the most suitable form of business organization for a company with a single owner.

However, one of the most important ways that this limited liability is maintained in any court proceedings is the critically important non-co-mingling of personal and business funds. If you are going to set up your new franchise as a LLC, do not co-mingle your personal funds, with your business funds. Set up clearly delineated financial books and records for the company that are totally separate and apart from your personal financial data. Frankly, this is a requirement for any of the above business organization types, but it is the one that can bite you the worst if you don't have them set up separately and your operating as a LLC and you wind up in court.

Obviously, as you begin to set up your new business, you will need to consult with your legal advisor as to the best way to provide maximum benefit to you and your family with the absolute minimum risk to you in the process.

Do you understand the critically important need for "Control?"

When I bought my company back in 1984 one of the very first things that the soon-to-be-previous owner told me as I was preparing to become a new business President was, "Don't take on a partner, be sure you have operational and financial control of the business!" He had just spent the last 20 years as a 50/50 partner with someone with whom he had virtually nothing in common and for the most part, they never agreed on anything! A very tough way to live your life and run a business.

Someone has to be the boss. Someone has to be able to make the final decision. Someone has to have at least 51% control.

Believe me, that little 1% can make a huge difference in the overall success of your business in the long term, and the quality of your personal life as well.

Get control!

Do you understand how to deal with Banks?

Almost all companies have needs for additional capital at one time or another. There are many sources of funds-both debt and equity. Regardless of the source, you must tell your story in a way that makes sense. In order to do that there are several things you can do to make your relationship with your banker more effective:

- Put yourself in the banker's shoes.
- Understand what banks are looking for in a good borrowing relationship.
- Learn how to prepare when going to the bank.
- Understand how to communicate effectively with your financial partner

What will the Bank want from you?

When dealing with your financing partners, you have to be prepared. Don't come in empty-handed. Be prepared to explain your needs: what you need, why, how you propose to structure the obligation, and how you propose to do that which they are most interested in, repay the debt.

The bank will typically not require any paperwork from you that you should not already be using in management tools:

- Financial statements that are accurate and prepared by the 15th day following the close of business of the previous month.
- A Profit Plan projection for the upcoming year.
- A Cash Budget (with a backup list of assumptions for both the profit plan and the cash budget.)

What is your franchisor's history in your geographic area?

Startup capital is the absolute most difficult to get, and is a constant challenge for the new, aspiring franchisee. If you approach your banker and your concept has had a checkered history with them (lots of loans already in default) your chances of getting the money are slim to none. The good news is that there are alternative sources for financing new startups, which can get you into business and within a year or so, ready for a less expensive regular bank line of credit. The Business Backer is one such funding source and there are several others as well.

Don't surprise your banker (or other sources of financing). If there's a problem, let them know about it early on. They're much more willing to work with you then, rather than after the problem has become known to them and you have kept silent.

Keep good communications with your bank, even if you don't have any immediate needs. The more your banker knows about you and your business, the better it will be able to respond in a timely manner when a need does arise.

Be proactive in your communication. If your banker asks for a semiannual financial statement from you to track the business, give her one quarterly, and take a few minutes of her time to bring her up to date on what's happening as your business continues to grow.

Banks have lots of money to lend, and banks are all pursuing well-managed profitable companies. If you have such a company, be sure to solicit multiple banks as you come to the renewal of your line of credit. You may be surprised at what service offerings are available to you in the marketplace today.

On the other hand, don't just shop for the cheapest deal in bank-ing. That doesn't always give you the long-term added value that a good (and perhaps somewhat more expensive) bank can provide you. The longer you do business with the same bank, the more they know about you, your business and your industry, and the better able it will be to serve your needs. And, when times get tough again, as they surely will, your banker will be much more likely to work with you if you have been with them for several years.

If you have a new banking relationship, insist that the bank visits your operation at least once a year. They can't understand your business by staying behind a desk in the bank!

Your banker is, in many ways, a partner in your business. Treat them as such-not as a foe. The same applies to your accountant, attorney, insurance expert and any other professional advisors that work with you to make your business more successful.

Finally, if you're not happy with your banking relationship ask other franchisees in your network about bankers. Who are they working with, how's the service, etc. Shop around. Once again, if you have a viable profitable business, you can be sure there's a bank that wants to do business with you.

What are the Five C's of Credit?

What do you think a banker looks for in a customer? Well, there are the five C's of credit that lay out the specific characteristics that the bank is looking for in a client. They are as follows:

1. Character

    • The history of the business and reputation in the community.
    • The resume of the new owner.
    • Both personal and business references.
    • A plan of succession to protect the bank's interests in case of an untimely accident

2. Capacity

    • Minimum debt service coverage of 1.25. In other words for every $1.00 of debt, the bank is looking for $1.25 of assets cover it.
    • Global cash flow (both business and personal) to fund the operation.
    • Projections/pro-forma financial guesstimates.
    • The key performance ratios of the industry. These should come from your franchisor and give you clear direction as to how the successful franchisees run their businesses.
    • Net worth of the owners.
    • Retained earnings growth if you're buying an existing franchise.
    • Working Capital.
    • A/R-A/P/Inventory Turnover (Cash Conversion Cycle)

3. Collateral

    • Appraised value to cost.
    • Equipment/rolling stock appraisal-evaluation.
    • Down payment.
    • Additional collateral-junior liens on real estate.

- Work in progress.
- Government contracts with guaranteed sales and payment periods.
- A/Rs Your receivables that are no more than 60 days past due

4. Capital

- Down payment.
- Subordination of debt: This is the debt that you borrowed from friends and family that can be subordinated and put into second position behind the bank loan and/or line of credit.
- Outside investors.
- Distributions

5. Conditions

- Volatility.
- Local, regional, state economy.
- Product replacement, improvement, or enhancement.
- Social-divorce or death.
- Business/stockholders, partners, ownership changes.
- Competition.
- Location

What are the Bankers three C's of Data?

In addition to the five C's of Credit, the bankers also have three C's of Data that are absolutely critical for you to be aware of as you are preparing your loan proposal for their review.

1. Complete

   - Complete income statement and balance sheet including a comparison to the annual plan.
   - A/R and A/P aging reports.
   - A monthly cash flow.
   - All extraordinary issues explained

2. Consistent

   - Prepared by a competent bookkeeper using appropriate accounting tools.
   - Formats and pagination are maintained throughout consistently each month.

3. Current

   - Monthly is the new minimum standard.
   - If you are in trouble, weekly can be required.

What are the Bankers "Red Flags" that, in general, prevent them from approving a loan?

As you can imagine, banks also have, from bitter loan experience, very specific issues that, when they see them in a business, raise immediate red flags and lead to that awful word "No." If you're looking to purchase an operating franchise that has any of these characteristics, you will have a definite uphill climb towards financing the transaction.

1. The business doesn't make money.
2. Inadequate, infrequent or inaccurate financial statements.

3. Hurried loan request.
4. Unclear, poorly thought out loan purpose.
5. Rapid, unusual inventory buildup.
6. Uncontrolled, unmanaged growth.
7. Inadequate cash flow and coverage of existing debt service.
8. A thinly capitalized operation where the current ratio is less than two to one.
9. Poor or marginal personal credit scores.
   Poor   = sub 650
   Marginal = sub 680
10. High Accounts Receivable concentration: If any one customer is greater than 20% of the total sales.
11. No three-year financial spread analysis.
12. The owners don't understand or use benchmarking for financial analysis.
13. Owners don't understand or know their key performance indicators.
14. Multiple entities that are not clearly divided for profit and loss and cash flow purposes.
15. Starting/buying a business with no previous background.
16. Any significant management change:
    a. Owners to kids or internal management transition: These transitions can be exceedingly challenging to a business and have caused many a loan default over the years.
    b. Significant owner health issues.

Any one of these characteristics will dramatically impact your ability to fund your franchise acquisition, so in addition to understanding the numbers, you also need to understand the history, culture and community reputation of the company you are considering.

Do you have, or understand the need for an Exit Strategy?

It's been said that the time to begin your exit strategy is the day that you buy your business. That is also totally pie-in-the-sky. The day you become a small business owner you are literally up to your neck in alligators and remain that way for much of your business career. For most of us, it's all we can do to get through planning for the week and/or month, much less the 15/20 year plan to sell.

However, when you get to a point where it is time to sell, a three-year plan is highly recommended.

Do you know how to prepare a business for sale?

Small business owners minimize taxes by stripping out all the profits of the business for themselves. While this is great for the business owner while they are operating the business, it is counterproductive for the owner when you're attempting to sell it for maximum value. Any bank that is going to finance the acquisition is looking for profitability, and no matter how well you craft a reconstructed pretax cash flow of the business, it is not the same as leaving cash in the business, in the bank. As we like to say in Profit Mastery, "Profit is an opinion; Cash is a fact."

In order to maximize value when you sell, you need to begin to leave something in place for the new owner to utilize as part of their buying process, most notably cash. You also need to be willing to pay more taxes because you're going to demonstrate true profitability by leaving more of the profits in the business.

In general, however this tactic will reward you in the long run by driving up the value of your business when it's time to find a buyer.

Do you understand the government regulations that franchisors operate under?

Franchising is one of the most highly regulated forms of business activity in the US. This is a result of an early history of franchisees investing in unethical networks that had as their sole purpose taking the franchisee's money and not caring if the franchisee could actually create a successful business.

Bowing to consumer demand, Congress set up a series of over 30 agencies to regulate the franchising process and to protect franchisees. In spite of all of this effort, there are still many stories of franchisees that invest their life savings, give it a good run for two or three years and wind up disillusioned, sometimes divorced and broke.

Unfortunately, still today there are franchise networks whose business plan is thinly disguised, churn the franchise location every three years, with a new franchise fee, new owner, continuing royalty payments on the sales with absolutely no concern as to what happens to the profitability.

Where do you eat?

Remember: Your franchisor eats off the top line of your sales, and you pay him/her a royalty payment every month based on your revenue.

You, on the other hand, live, eat, and support your family on the bottom line profitability of the business and that's where you need to focus your efforts to understand how the business actually makes a profit.

The Federal Trade Commission (FTC) requires that every franchisor provide to a prospective franchisee their FDD. Bear in mind, that this is a document that is designed to ultimately convince you to buy their franchise, so as with all information, it needs to be reviewed with a very critical eye.

As this chapter is focused primarily on the financial part of the FDD, I will concentrate on:

Item 19: Financial Performance Representations.

Frankly, there are few things more infuriating to me than the typical Item 19 provided in a FDD. It brings to mind the old governmental adage, 'If you're trying to obscure financial data for the general public, hide it with columns and rows, and columns and rows, and columns and rows, and columns and rows, etc., ad infinitum.

The most recent Item 19 I reviewed contained a total of 14 pages of financial data, 95% of which was, for all intents and purposes, completely useless to a prospective franchisee. "Amount and distribution of annual sales between company-owned units and franchised, upper range average, middle range average, lower range average," is quite frankly a little concern to the new franchisee.

What are the two most critical numbers for your new business?

The two most important numbers that you need to understand for your new business are Break-even and Gross Margin. Simply defined, Gross Margin is the total of your sales minus your cost of goods sold and production labor. Here is a rule of thumb you can take to the bank. If the franchise operation that you're looking at is not going to deliver to you a Gross Margin of at least 40%, walk.

Unfortunately, the typical Item 19 does not provide you Gross Margin information, only net operating profits. And, as we have observed franchise networks preparing their Item 19s, this number can be dramatically "massaged", "averaged", "common sized", etc.!

To achieve a net operating profit, you must have a strong Gross Margin to be able to cover your general and operating expenses. If the Item 19 you are reviewing in the FDD you have received from your franchisor does not include Gross Margin calculations, then you need to request actual GAAP (Generally Accepted Accounting Principles) based financial statements that do provide Gross Margin data.

Does the franchisor know if their franchisees are profitable?

Here is another ugly little secret. Many franchise networks have no idea whether or not their franchisees are actually making any money. They receive a royalty check and the sales report at the end of every month, and that is it. This is the "old school" model of franchise operations, and frankly as long as the royalty checks keep coming in, the franchisor doesn't really concern themselves with whether or not the unit is actually profitable. Beware of such franchise networks.

Look for networks that can deliver to you actual financial information about their franchisees monthly profitability. Hopefully in the form of an *actual* financial statement submitted to the franchisor through a benchmark study report produced by an independent third party that delivers back to the network comprehensive financial information regarding the profitability of the network.

Does your franchisor Benchmark their network at least biannually?

These benchmark studies are invaluable tools for a prospective franchisee. In general, they lay out the low, median and high-performing franchisees and deliver solid management data as to how the top performers are managing their companies. Ask the franchisor you are considering for their benchmark study and see what happens.

As a new franchisee, your single most important goal is to get your new business to break-even, where your sales are covering all of your expenses, as quickly as possible. This enables you to stop writing checks every month for the pleasure of doing whatever it is you decided to do and takes the operation from being a very expensive hobby, to one that's actually a functioning business, ready to contribute profits to you and your family.

As you proceed down the road toward becoming a new franchisee, be sure to ask for specific references from franchisees that are already in the system or willing to talk about their financial success.

The franchisor will be willing to give you these references. As you talk with them,
I encourage you to ask these franchisees for references as well, trying to dig deeper into the network. The franchisee you want to talk to is one who has not been as successful, and it's important that you try to understand why. Are they disgruntled with the system? Did they not implement the process that they purchased? These questions are extremely important for you as a prospective franchisee, because they lay out for you what your future may look like if things don't go smoothly between you and your franchisor.

Understanding how your franchisor deals with the marginally successful unit and brings them up to profitable operations is important, as that may very well be you a year from now.

Can you give information regarding actual, average and projected CASH FLOW, SALES, and PROFITS.

You may ask why I put Cash Flow first, instead of Sales and Profits. It goes like this: The rookie is concerned about sales first, profit second, and cash flow a distant third.

The seasoned business manager is concerned first about cash flow, then sales and finally profits. It's cash that actually pays the bills and allows you to stay in business. So what are the things that you need to ask your franchisor about cash flow?

Does your business model have a seasonal sales pattern?

It begins with understanding the seasonality of the sales pattern of your business model. Virtually every business has a seasonal pattern and that pattern dramatically impacts your ability to pay your bills and sustain the business over the course of a full 12 months. Carefully review the seasonality of the business and prepare a month-by-month cash flow projection that will help you understand that pattern. You will need this cash flow statement as part of your loan package that you will need to help fund the start-up of the business.

What is the typical Accounts Receivable collections period for your network?

The second critical piece of cash flow is how quickly you collect your receivables. It's reasonable to assume that unless you're in some type of food service industry where your customers pay as they receive their food, it is highly likely that you will be billing your commercial accounts and collecting receivables over time.

This collections time is absolutely critical to understand as you are preparing your cash flow statement. It is important to know that the difference between collecting receivables in 30 days and 60 days can be dramatic to your business's fiscal health and your family's fortunes.

In many industries, the collections time is actually set by the vendor and there is nothing you can do to change it. Understanding that and its impact on your business model is another important piece for you to know before purchasing your franchise.

In Profit Mastery we teach the critically important concept of "the value of ONE day" in the collections process. Understanding best practices for collecting your receivables in your network is absolutely critical to your cash flow success.

Can you give information regarding actual, average and projected SALES?

One of the most important assets that you were purchasing from your franchisor is their sales and marketing plan that will drive business into your establishment. The branding, marketing, national positioning and overall sales support provided by your network is absolutely critical to your success. Asking the franchisees about the effectiveness of this support is one of the most important questions on your list.

Understanding the first year of sales ramp-up in your new location is extremely important. Where will the sales come from?

What percentage of revenue will come from what accounts?

If you discover that your network has 80% of its sales in two or three key accounts, this significantly raises your risk as a new franchisee.

Can you give information regarding actual, average and projected PROFITS?

As I said previously, often many franchise networks do not actually know what the profitability is of their franchisees. It is highly likely that your profitability questions will need to be answered by the franchisees already in the network, not by the franchisor representatives.

In Profit Mastery we teach that there are only four ways to drive the profits. They are:

1. Sell more units
2. Raise the price of the units you already sell
3. Control/reduce your variable costs
4. Control/reduce your fixed costs

How well the concept you have selected allows you to do each of the above items will directly affect your ability to generate profits.

For example, if your network requires you to adhere to nationally set pricing, and your expenses are geographically higher than the rest of your network, you already begin your business journey with a significant handicap.

Understanding how you can manage each of the above four items directly affects your ability to generate profits in your new business.

In summation:

The 23 years I spent as the President of my own company where some of the most wonderful, challenging, rewarding, frustrating, terrifying years of my life, and I am so grateful that I had the experience. You have embarked upon that same journey, and I applaud and support you in your efforts.

Successful, profitable, small, family-owned businesses are the foundation of our entire economy, and while I may have sounded discouraging in my comments regarding certain franchisors, in truth, buying a franchise is one of the best ways to get into business as they say, "For Yourself, But Not By Yourself."

Choose your franchisor partner wisely.

Questions You Should Ask Your Financial Advisor:
NOTE: you will see that each heading throughout this chapter has been worded as a question. So, in addition to the headings-as-questions, see the following:

- Looking at the franchise I wish to buy, and looking at my personal financial resources, and in addition to the franchisor's qualification standard, does it appear that I have the personal resources to buy this franchise without sacrificing my personal standard of living?
- Are there any "landmines" that I need to be aware of?
- I am sure you are willing to prepare a business plan for me. However, I may learn more if I do it myself, with your guidance. Can you help me with this?
- If the franchisor doesn't provide bookkeeping software, can you recommend one?
- Should I do the bookkeeping and then have monthly financial statements prepared by a CPA? (You don't want

to pay a CPA to do bookkeeping).
- Can you help me with preparing a loan package for my bank? For an SBA loan?
- Looking at the financial statements provided in Item 21 of the FDD and the number of outlets in Item 20 of the FDD, is there any way to determine what the average revenues are for this franchise network?
- If there is an Item 19 Financial Performance Representation, can you help me evaluate and interpret it? Can I make enough money to reach my personal financial goals?
- When the time comes that I need to sell my franchise, will you help me maximize my equity? At what point should I start preparing for the sale of my business?
- After review of the FDD, what else should I ask the franchise sales representative? What specifically do you suggest that I ask the franchisees?

Next, Questions you should ask your Franchise Consultant.

* * * * *

 Rod Bristol is the Senior Vice President of **Profit Mastery** in Seattle, Washington, and is part of the team that promotes the expansion of the Profit Mastery program nationally and internationally. Rod began his career as an investment banker in Seattle, doing mergers and acquisitions in the $2 million to $20 million dollar middle-market. Highlights of his career included being elected to the White House Conference on Small Business, and served as Governor Appointee and Chairman of the Washington State Economic Development Finance Authority and Small Busi-ness Improvement Council. Rod is a Certified Franchise Executive, has a Bachelor of Arts degree from the University of Washington.

CHAPTER 8

Questions You Should Ask A Franchise Consultant

"To win takes a complete commitment of mind and body. When you can't make that commitment, they don't call you a champion anymore."
—Rocky Marciano

Many people go into a franchise business search with no clue about what kind of business they want to start. With today's technology, you can easily search "franchising", or visit a few franchise websites and peruse through hundreds of franchise opportunities. There are about 3700 franchises available and it can be easy to get overwhelmed with all the options and information.

It is so important to you align yourself with a franchise that will give you the best chance for success. There are a lot of great franchises out there that offer a wealth of support, but, like any other industry, there are a few "bad apples". How do you pick which franchises to research? How will you know which ones will best match your skill set? How will you know which franchises have the potential to meet your business and financial goals? This is where bringing in the expertise of a franchise consultant, like me, can be very valuable to you. Here are some questions you should consider when working with a franchise consultant:

What is a franchise consultant and how can they help me with my franchise search?

A franchise consultant is someone who acts as a "guide" to help you navigate the franchise industry and to match you to the best possible franchise to meet your personal and business goals. One of the best analogies for a franchise consult is that they work much like a real-estate agent does. Think back to when you bought your last house. You probably found a real-estate agent and provided them all the parameters for what you wanted in a home. You told them the area you wanted to live in, your price range, the number of bedrooms you needed, the types of amenities you preferred, and so on. After taking all your information, the real-estate agent lined up a list of houses for you to preview. They probably found out what other homes had sold for in the area and educated you on the process of purchasing a home. Once you had found the house of your dreams, the real-estate agent put together an offer to purchase and tried to get you your best deal. Once your offer on the house was accepted, the real-estate agent then guided you through the home inspection (they often have people to whom they can refer you) and they may have even helped you work with a local bank for financing. Ultimately, they guided you through all the steps to closing and purchasing your new home.

A franchise consultant works the same way. They will find out things like: Why do you want to start a business? What does your skill-set include? What are your interests? How much money do you have to invest? What kind of income do you need to eventually earn? Where you would like to operate your business?
After learning about you, they will go out and research potential franchise "fits" and present you with options that meet your criteria. Once they have presented you with franchises for your consideration, they will then prepare for you the process of investigating a franchise. A good franchise consultant will also provide

you with valuable educational resources along the way. In addition, you will probably need some sort of funding, so a franchise consultant should have relationships with funding companies to aid you with the financial aspect. Once you complete your franchise due diligence and choose the right business for you, then the franchise consultant will prepare you for approval by the franchise and for the legal process of signing a franchise agreement. As a franchise consultant, I will have my clients work with a franchise attorney (another resource I refer) to review the agreement and make sure everything is in order before signing their agreement and officially buying the franchise.

How much does it cost to hire a franchise consultant?

A franchise consultant should never charge you a fee. Their fee is paid by the franchisor once you sign the franchise agreement. Let's refer back to our real-estate agent example: a real-estate agent represents you to get you the best deal on a home and when they are successful and you close on your house, their fee is paid by Seller, not you. A franchise consult works the same way, with their fee coming from the Franchisor. As a franchise consultant, I often will refer to myself as a "buyer's agent" as I represent my clients to get them the deal that is best for their particular needs.

How do I know if my franchise consultant is only showing me franchises that pay them a higher fee vs. franchises that will meet my goals?

This is a great question to ask a franchise consultant. A good franchise consultant should tell you they request the same fee from every franchisor for placing a client into their franchise. This way you are ensured that it doesn't matter which franchise you pick - that consultant will get the same fee no matter what.

Can I get a discount on a franchise fee if I go directly to the franchise instead of using a franchise consultant?

Simply stated, no. Franchises are required by law to provide you a Franchise Disclosure Document (FDD), which will state their franchise fee to buy their franchise and rights to their name and operating system. They can't change, or discount, that franchise fee if you are referred to a franchise through a franchise consultant. Frankly, many franchises prefer to work with candidates that are referred through a franchise consultant as a franchise consultant has already pre-screened the candidate to ensure they have the skill-set and meet the financial requirements for their franchise. Also, a franchise consultant preps a candidate on how to conduct a proper franchise investigation and provides that candidate many resources to aid them in their decision. Most franchisors will say that a candidate that works with a franchise consultant is usually *preferable* to work with, as they are a better-educated and pre-pared potential investor.

How long will it take me to investigate and find the right franchise?

A good franchisor will have a process to teach you about their fran-chise and complete all the research within 4-8 weeks. However, this will mean dedicating about 10-15 hours a week per franchise you are investigating during that period to meet that timeline. Of course, at the end of the process you and the franchisor should be determining whether you are moving ahead or not. So, the timeline will really depend on YOU. Over the years, I have worked with a variety of people in all different stages of their career. Some of my clients have been laid off and they don't want to go back to working for someone else, so they tend to want to move faster to find the right business and have the time to dedicate to research-ing their next career move. Other clients I have worked with have had full time jobs and are looking for a business they can manage semi-passively so they can have the extra income of a business while they are still working. While other clients will tell me they no longer enjoy working for someone else, or are no longer growing in their career, so they want to explore transitioning from their job to business ownership. So, it could take a little longer to go through the process depending your work situation. I do caution my clients that if, during the time they are working with a franchisor, they are not showing a franchisor that they are consistently making progress and completing the action items that the franchisor requests in a timely manner, that more than likely, the franchise will start to think they are not a serious investor. Your lack of progress could be interpreted by the franchisor that you have a lack of interest, and this could result in the franchise stopping the process with you and never offering you a franchise.

Don't forget that investigating a franchise is a two-way street...you are interviewing the franchise to make sure it is the right fit for you, and they are interviewing you to ensure you can follow a process and will be a good franchisee that can represent their brand well in the marketplace. The best thing to do is be prepared to take time each week for your investigation. If you think you will move a little slower during certain steps of the investigation process, or that you may take you longer due to work or personal obligations, then you need to communicate that upfront. Sometimes, based on your timeframe, a franchise may suggest you hold off starting the investigation process with them until you have more time to dedicate to learning about their opportunity.

On the flip side, no one should be rushing you through your franchise investigation. If things are moving too fast or you are feeling pushed through the steps by a franchise, you need to communicate that to your franchise consultant. A good consultant will communicate on your behalf to the franchise and let them know they need to slow down. Again, you are making a major investment and your franchise consultant should ensure that you have the time to "turn over all the rocks" and get all your questions answered so you can make a sound business decision.

How does my franchise consultant ensure the franchises they are presenting to me are solid business models with good track records?

Unfortunately, many "franchise consultants" do not screen the franchisors to make sure they are "playing by the rules: and have happy and successful franchisees. You need to ask your franchise consultant what process they take in screening franchises. Let's not forget, there are 3700 franchises and there are some 'bad apples'. A successful franchise system should provide a lot of support, such as: training, marketing and operations. And, as a result, those franchisors should have several successful owners.
At *The You Network*, we take the process of researching franchises very seriously. We get called by 40-50 franchisors a month that would like for us to represent their franchise concept to our clients. However, before we would even consider presenting their franchise to one of our clients, they have to pass the scrutiny of our Brand Committee. Our Brand Committee, consisting of our most experienced consultants, will read through their Franchise Disclosure Document to ensure their franchise meets all Federal and State laws, as certain states have some special requirements that have to be met. If the franchisor cites any litigation in the FDD, our committee investigates that litigation to make sure this franchise is "playing by the rules." Some of the people on our Brand Committee have been CFO's for some major franchises so they review the financials of the franchise to ensure they are financially sound. Finally, the most important people on our committee are the ones that call the franchisees within that franchise system. They ask those franchisees numerous "validation" questions, such as: "Did they get the support and training they were promised? Are they happy with the franchisor? Are they making the kind of

money they thought they would make? If they had the chance to do this all over again, would they?" If, and only if, we hear a lot of positive feedback by the majority of franchisees, and we see that they are financially and legally sound, then we know we have a franchise we can present to one of our clients. Interestingly, as all of our prospective clients also "validate" with franchise owners when they are investigating a franchise, they continue to provide us with feedback – and we also "drop" a franchise from our portfolio should they not maintain performance standards.

Bottom line, you are about to put your hard-earned money into a major business investment, and if your franchise consultant doesn't "vet" the franchises they are showing you, then you need to find another consultant.

How do I know I have found the right franchise consultant?

This is a VERY important question! You are about to make a major investment and a life-changing decision, so make sure you get a franchise consultant whose priority is about YOU and YOUR needs. There are numerous groups out there that call themselves franchise consultants or franchise coaches, but many of them have had little-to-no experience in franchising, and are really no more than "brokers."

Ask them a few of these questions to learn about their experience:

- How many years have you been in franchising?

- Have you ever worked for a franchise company and, if so, in what capacity?

- Have you ever owned your own business?

- How many people have you assisted getting into business?

If the so-called 'franchise consultant' has never worked in franchising or owned a business, you may want to question whether they are going to have the expertise to guide you on the journey to business ownership. Also, question the process they are going to take to learn about you and present you appropriate franchises. If they are going to try and present you franchises after a short 30-minute call then this person isn't a true franchise consultant, but just someone looking to make a commission off of you. At *The You Network*, we have you first complete a profile that will provide both us and you with helpful tools for matching you to the right businesses. We even have tools to test your core competencies, and what motivates you as an investor. Understand, there is a bit of a 'science' to helping you find the right business, so it is crucial to collect as much information as we can to help us better determine the types of businesses or industry you would most likely thrive in. Also, we spend several hours going over your profile with you and asking you questions to ensure we understand who YOU are and what is important to YOU. Interestingly, some of the most experienced business people tell us that they wished they had found us earlier in their business search as they realize without our expertise they may have made some serious errors in choosing the right business.

And finally, a franchise consultant with a lot of experience in franchising has probably made a lot of connections in the franchise industry. A seasoned franchise consultant is not only going to be able to provide you resources like franchise attorneys and funding companies BUT they are also going to use their connections to help you get into a franchise. Let me provide an example of how this is valuable to you: most franchisors will tell you they get hundreds of inquiries each month regarding their franchise opportunity. These franchisors will have to prioritize who they will spend time with, and, as a result, they don't always respond to all those inquiries. Similar to an executive recruiter, a franchise consultant with a lot of industry experience has probably worked with and built relationships with the founders and key executives at these franchise companies. This means if you have an interest in a particular franchise then that franchise consultant is going to call the key people at the franchisor and tell them how great you are and why you would make a wonderful franchisee for their system. This gets you to the "top of the list" at the franchise.

In closing, before you make a major investment and life-changing decision you should consider the services of a franchise consultant. They will act as your advocate to represent YOU and YOUR goals. This is just one more way to ensure that you have all the tools you need to make a sound business decision!

Note: The author of this section has included the questions you should ask into the body of the chapter. The author has suggested to you what questions are the most important to ask of a Franchise Consultant, with appropriate answers, of which you should also be aware.

* * * * *

Jenny Childs is currently a Vice President and Sr. Franchise Consultant at The You Network and creator of FranchiseYOU.

The You Network is a consortium of 20 senior-level franchise executives who are asked to join by "invitation only" and include some of the most seasoned consulting professionals in the franchising industry. Jenny works with people all over the United States and Canada to help them learn about franchising and to place them into a franchise where they will have the best chance for success. She is uniquely qualified to assist potential business investors as she has worked in all facets of franchising over the last 15 years including: franchise development, franchise operations and franchise funding. If you are interested in working with Jenny Childs or learning more about her services she can be contacted at http://www.FranchiseYOU.com

CHAPTER 9

Questions The Franchisor Should be Asking YOU

Knowledge itself is power.
—Francis Bacon

This just in... did you know that there are some franchisors that will sell *anyone* a franchise? I will not say that they are un-ethical, but I will say that they would not meet the standard of "awarding franchises" to *only* qualified persons who meet the financial, cultural and work background requirements. There is a joke among long-time franchise people that talk about franchisors who will sell a franchise to anyone who passes the "mirror test". If you don't know what the "mirror test" is, well, position your nose about an inch away from a mirror, and exhale a big breath. If there is a patch of fog (condensation) on the mirror, you passed!

Yes, as noble as *most* franchisors are about making sure that they "award franchises" to the right people, there are still those franchisors that will basically sell a franchise (license) to anyone who has the money. Sad, but true. I only say this because after 25 years of socializing with Franchise Development people and the coaches/consultants who certainly "talk the talk", I have person-ally put myself through the franchise sales process as a BUYER and found that after one single interview, I was sent the FDD along with the (post-dated) Franchise Agreements with my name already filled in and little sticky notes attached with "sign here" in all of the appropriate, designated lines, complete with instructions on what day I should sign, date and return (with check, of course). Yes, I personally experienced it!

We have all experienced that "gut feeling" when something just doesn't feel right. Like when you are being pressured to make a hasty decision. If you are being pressured, walk away! That should be a major red flag.

I have also personally witnessed a VERY respectable franchisor that has quite an impressive dog and pony show (Discovery Day), where prospects are told, "not to bring their checkbooks, no pressure to buy while you are here". True, but even though a check will not pass hands, you certainly *will be pressured* to make a verbal commitment, "on a scale of 1-10". Especially after that impressive show.

I have also seen tactics of "buy soon before the franchise fee increases (especially at the end of the year). Or "buy soon while you can still get the less expensive build out / equipment package".

I am not a fan of pressure tactics. I may be from the old school, but I also do not believe in selling a franchise to anyone who walks through the door with the necessary amount of money. I have had to personally deny selling a franchise to an overly qualified individual (required, verifiable financial resources to buy the franchise was around $180,000-200,000. He had over $8 million, liquid). I had to deny him because he could not make the necessary sales calls needed to make the business grow. When he thought he could "hire that function", he was told that it would skew the financial model. Wow. Not too many franchisors would walk away from that kind of money.

There should be a *qualification process*. In the franchise world, most franchisors stress that they do not sell a franchise to every-one who walks through the door with the appropriate amount of funding. The qualification process certainly includes ensuring the applicant has the necessary financial resources. Actually, that is the first level. Because if you cannot financially qualify, the fact that you are a cultural fit, and that there is a location available are both moot points.

Back in Chapter 3, we discussed the initial interview. We prepared you for how to answer those questions. Now, we share with you what question should be asked *of* you. What the franchisor is seeking is to *qualify you*. They need to ask enough questions of you to determine:

- If you have the **Financial Resources.**
- If you have the **Skill set.**
- If you have a **Passion for the business.**
- If you are a **Culture Fit** (probably determined at a later date, but they are trying to assess you on the initial call).
- If you know **what it will take to be successful** in their model.
- Your **goals.**
- If you have **family support**.

So, with this in mind, here is an extensive sampling of questions that *should* be asked of you in the initial interview.

- Describe your work history fro the past 10 years.
- What were your responsibilities?
- What as made you successful in your career?
- What accomplishments are you most proud of?
- In what areas do you know you will need additional training or support in owning your own business?

- What did you like most about what you were doing? Why?
- Looking back at your career/work history, what would you have changed? Why?
- Are you married? What does your spouse think about you starting a business?
- Do you have children? What are their ages? What do they think?
- In what area (geography) are you looking to start a business?
- How will you family be involved in this franchise?
- To whom will you look to for guidance/advice in making your decision?
- What especially has caught your eye about our concept?
- What other concepts have you looked at?
- What has kept you from moving forward with these concepts?
- Why is now the time to start your own business?
- What goals are you looking to accomplish next in your life? Why does it matter?
- And why is that important to you?
- What will be the result if these goals are not accomplished?
- What are you doing now to accomplish your goals?
- Why do you think you will be a success in this concept?
- What is your personal income goal for the next: 1 year? 3 years? 5+ years?
- How much cash does it take each month to run your household?
- What is your annual income now? (Or with your past job)?
- Are you looking to replace that number? Exceed it? If it is less, will that be ok?
- How will your household expenses be covered while you

are starting your business?

- What amount of cash do you have ready to invest in this business today? In 90 days?
- Excluding items such as cars and furniture, and only including things like cash, savings, home equity and 401(k)'s, how much would you estimate your net worth to be?
- If you find that after going through our Discovery process, that you will have the opportunity to affordably accomplish your goals, what are you going to do?
- When would you like for your business to be open?
- Where will you get the funds to start?
- Think about "pulling the trigger" on this opportunity. How do you feel about investing the money, time, energy heart & soul into starting your own business?
- Can you see yourself owning this type of business?

Well, we have come full circle. In the first chapter, I gave you an extensive list of questions you should ask *yourself*. If you answered those questions honestly, then of course it made sense to proceed to each subsequent chapter through the sales process, so to speak. And now we find ourselves rehearsing questions that will be asked of you by the franchisor, or franchise consultant. There is no doubt that you certainly will be asking a lot of questions during the process. However, regardless of who is asking, the best questions are still those asked of you! And if you know the answers to those questions, they will be the best ones to guide you to the answers you ask of others!

Conclusion / Miscellaneous Notes

(some of which are important)

*"All our dreams can come true, if we have the courage
to pursue them."*
—Walt Disney

As stated earlier, buying a franchise is not for everyone. But if you think it is for you, hopefully I have given you enough questions to prepare yourself for the process. There are a couple of subjects that are not addressed in the previous chapters that might be worth at least mentioning so you don't think they are forgotten.

One of them is the mention of **registration states**. There are 13 registration states in the United States in which the franchisor must be registered and file their FDD with the Secretary of State in order to sell franchises in that state. Because this book is targeted to all of the United States and the English-speaking world, it would not be appropriate to dedicate much space to registration states. However, this would be a good reason to engage the services of a franchise consultant (see Chapter 8). To determine if you live in a registration state, you can always go to the IFA website (www.franchise.org), consult with your franchise attorney, or simply conduct an Internet search "franchise registration states".

The other subject is the subject of **discovery day**. The reason why I did not address discovery day in the book is because so many different franchisors conduct discovery day in so many different ways. Many of them do not look for a commitment to move forward with purchase and yet many more do. Another reason is because if you make it as far as attending discovery day, you probably would have asked all the crucial questions presented in this book during the process itself, prior to attending discovery day. Many of the most important questions *should* have already been asked. And discovery day is simply the final step in the process before signing the agreement. Most (if not *all*) of your due diligence should have already been conducted. My only word of warning about discovery day would be to pay attention to see if you're being pressured. And of course, as I have stated before, I am not a fan of pressure tactics. If you feel that you are being pressured into a decision, you should postpone your decision (unless you have already committed and made the decision to do so). Basically, my feeling is that discovery day really isn't part of the *due diligence* process. It is a step in the *sales* process. But it really is more of the franchisor's desire to *meet* you before entering into the agreement *with* you.

I wish you the best of luck in your discovery process. If you decide to move forward with buying a franchise, I certainly hope that I have given you the tools to become more successful. If you have any questions of any kind, please contact me through the website: www.franchisevalidator.com. Wishing you great success!